The Story of the Cathedral of the Madeleine

Gary Topping

Fig. 1: Detail of Cathedral ceiling.

The Story of the Cathedral of the Madeleine

Gary Topping

Archivist of the Roman Catholic Diocese
of Salt Lake City

sagebrush
PRESS

Images on color plates, chapter headings and
pages ii, vii, 87 and 95: © 2009 Ann Torrence
Images on pages 74 and 98: © 1992 Zeke McCabe.
All other images are courtesy of the archives of the Diocese of Salt Lake City.

Published by Sagebrush Press
Salt Lake City, Utah 84105

ISBN 978-0-9703130-6-5
Library of Congress Control Number: 2009931950

Printed in the United States of America.
First Printing, Summer 2009

to Bernice Maher Mooney

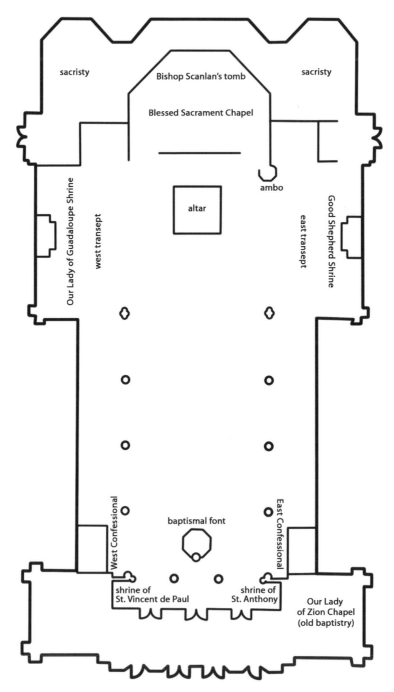

Fig. 2: Floor plan of the Cathedral of the Madeleine in 2009

Contents

Foreword by Bishop John C. Wester   ix
Preface and Acknowledgments   xiii

1. Creation   1
   Beginnings of Utah Catholicism; St. Mary's Church; Bishop
   Lawrence Scanlan; designing and building the Cathedral of the
   Madeleine

2. Transformation   21
   Bishop Joseph S. Glass and the redecoration of the Cathedral
   interior

3. Redemption   41
   Bishops John J. Mitty and James E. Kearney; the Great Depression,
   and retirement of the Cathedral debt; Bishop Duane G. Hunt;
   World War II; and the emergence of modern Utah Catholicism

4. Restoration   59
   Bishop Joseph Lennox Federal; the Second Vatican Council; and
   the exterior restoration of the Cathedral

5. Renovation   75
   Bishop William K. Weigand and the interior renovation; charitable
   and cultural programs in the new Cathedral

Color Plates by Ann Torrence   after 46
Endnotes   99
Index   107

Fig. 3: Carving at the railing of the ambo or pulpit.

Foreword

There is something about a cathedral. To know what I mean, just drop by the Cathedral of the Madeleine some afternoon when the sun is in earnest about making the end of the day. The shafts of light filtering through the stained glass windows seem to highlight the lengthening shadows, giving a peaceful hue to the softly colored walls and murals. It is awesomely quiet yet one can hear the city sounds gently wafting through the cracks between the front doors. There is always a lingering odor of beeswax and incense that reminds you of the importance of sign and symbol in the sacred liturgies that have just ended or perhaps concluded decades ago. As a matter of fact, as you settle into this serene setting, your imagination will bring you back one hundred years so that you can hear the echoes of Bishop Scanlan offering the dedication Mass; Archbishop Glennon of St. Louis preaching the homily on faith and family; Cardinal Gibbons of Baltimore delivering his beautiful tribute to our first shepherd, whom he called "the good bishop" or any number of Cathedral rectors and priests stirring their listeners to utter a fervent response of gratitude to a loving and compassionate God. Indeed, this wonderful cathedral, with its tree-like columns and green-sprouting capitals will convince you that you are walking in the cool afternoon shade with God at your side because this holy site, this sacred ground, is indeed the New Eden.

There really is something about a cathedral. It is not simply a museum of memories and artifacts but a living, dynamic house of worship that slumbers when empty and comes alive when God's holy people file into its pews. It seems to have had a life and will of its own as it moved from Second East to its current promontory on South Temple and as it underwent extensive renovation under Bishop Glass and then much later, Bishop Weigand. But these are mainly architectural and artistic realities that only begin to touch the real life of the cathedral as a link between God and humankind. The Cathedral of the Madeleine is a metaphor or sign of God's grace that initiates, confirms, sustains and nourishes His holy people. It is itself an image of the Body of Christ whose sole purpose is to sustain the living stones who gather with Christ, their head, day after day, Sunday after Sunday. One gets the impression that the Cathedral, imitating the faithful, is proud of the water splashed on its floors as babies and converts are baptized in its baptismal font, of the chrism smeared on its walls during its dedication one hundred years ago, and of the ambo and altar standing as witnesses to the life they hold in Word and Sacrament, proclaimed and celebrated year after year throughout the past century. In understated simplicity, the *cathedra* symbolizes the unity of this local Church of the Diocese of Salt Lake City as the laity, religious and clergy gather with their bishop to celebrate the sacred mysteries. Yes, this building is truly alive.

There is just something about a cathedral. Perhaps James Joyce expresses this reality best in his description of the Catholic Church: here comes everybody! If every person passing through the Cathedral's doors signed a guest book, we would have thousands and thousands of such volumes. Sacramental celebrations, prayer services, concerts, wedding practices, funerals, award ceremonies, graduations, retreats, civic gatherings, installations, ordinations and quiet prayer all call people from every walk of life to spend time in this hallowed edifice. During the day, the light streaming through the stained glass reminds the cathedral that it cannot stand alone: it depends on that which is outside it to enhance its beauty. During the night, however, the larger community is reminded of the place of the Cathedral in its day to day existence, giving it a deeper sense of beauty, wonder, awe and mystery. The Cathedral of the Madeleine has earned its place in the life of the people of Utah and is cherished by those of all faiths, cultures and traditions. It makes God mercifully immanent and at the same time awesomely transcendent as no other building can do. In this sense, the Cathedral is a revolving door through which heaven bound pilgrims can find rest, nourishment and peace along the way.

Dr. Gary Topping has captured well the essence of our beautiful Cathedral of the Madeleine. Building on the fine work of Bernice Mooney, he has given us a treasure in this historical record of a cathedral that has turned one hundred years old. This new work will stand with the recently revised *Salt of the Earth* as an enticing invitation to delve deeper into the rich tapestry of the history of our diocese, so intertwined with our mother church. I thank Dr. Topping for his splendid addition to our archives and I am confident that the reader will discover that, indeed, there is something wonderful about a cathedral, and particularly, the Cathedral of the Madeleine.

Bishop John C. Wester
Diocese of Salt Lake City

Fig. 4: Carl Neuhausen's original plan included spires that were never built.

Preface
and Acknowledgements

When Bernice Maher Mooney's *The Story of the Cathedral of the Madeleine* appeared in 1981, it was a landmark event in the historiography of Utah Catholicism. Other than a few welcome but sporadic periodical articles, it was the first substantial contribution to the thin historical literature of the Diocese of Salt Lake City since Father Louis Fries's diocesan history written to celebrate the ordination of Bishop John J. Mitty in 1926. As such, it was a particular kind of book. Since there was no recent diocesan history, her book, organized by successive episcopal administrations, included often extensive biographies of the bishops and narratives of the development of as many as she could of their programs emanating outward from the Cathedral to the diocese. Thus a large part of the great value of the book lay not only in its still unsurpassed account of the art, architecture, and history of the building, but in its peripheral glimpses into diocesan doings as well. The book was received with the enthusiasm it deserved, and has achieved the status of a classic of Utah historical literature.

Almost thirty years later, though, the book, like we human beings who were around to cheer its arrival, has begun to show its age. Concluding with the ordination of Bishop William K. Weigand, *The Story of the Cathedral of the Madeleine* of course does not cover the great interior renovation accomplished during his tenure, nor the formation of the Madeleine Choir School, the Madeleine Festival of the Arts and Humanities, the Eccles Organ concerts, and other dramatic developments of our own day. In addition, historical research on the Cathedral and the diocese has continued, indeed accelerated, since the book appeared, and those new discoveries and interpretations need to be incorporated. That accumulated literature, including *Salt of the Earth: The History of the Catholic Church in Utah, 1776–1987*, authored by Bernice with Msgr. Jerome C. Stoffel, with its successive revisions up to 2008, provided an even more monumental scope. No longer does a history of the Cathedral have to explain events elsewhere in the diocese except as needed for context or consequence. Now new research and fresh interpretations and subsequent events can be presented with a tight focus on the history of the building itself.

When Diocesan Vicar General Msgr. J. Terrence Fitzgerald passed on to me an inquiry from Cathedral Rector Msgr. Joseph M. Mayo wondering if I would be willing to revise and update Bernice's book as part of the 2009 celebration of the Cathedral centennial, I at first demurred. One does not tamper with a classic. But when, for various reasons including her recent completion of an arduous updating (in collaboration with Msgr. Fitzgerald) of *Salt of the Earth*, Bernice felt unable to undertake the project and encouraged me to attempt it, I finally agreed.

I have tried to retain as much of her work as was still valid and compatible with my own vision of what the new history should be. But I have freely made so many departures from the original conception and scope of her book, both because my interpretations of aspects of the history of the Cathedral occasionally vary from hers, and because of the changed circumstances within which I write, as described above, I take full responsibility for its contents. I have veered so far from the steady course she set that I have decided, out of fairness to her legacy, that my name alone would stand on the title page.

One of my biggest departures is the organizational scheme of the book. Bernice organized hers chronologically around the contributions of each successive bishop. While I retain a chronological organization, I have tried to divert as much attention as possible from the bishops, and to focus instead on the Cathedral building itself; the architects and artists who designed, built, and decorated it; the people who have worshipped there; and the liturgies and other programs that have taken place there. In making that choice, I place myself within the democratizing trend that has characterized Roman Catholicism since the Second Vatican Council of the 1960s. No longer do we think of bishop and church as one and the

Fig. 5: The organ in 2009.

same, nor of church history as a succession of bishops' biographies, any more than we would write a history of the United States focusing only on presidential administrations.

On the other hand, this book does contain a great deal of material on the bishops. A cathedral is, after all, a bishop's church. Everything that takes place in a cathedral must be approved by the bishop if indeed it is not initiated by him. A cathedral can quite legitimately be many different things, and what it happens to be at a particular time depends heavily on the personality, the gifts, and the ministerial orientation of the bishop at that time. Thus I have given often extensive coverage of a bishop's background, personality, training, and interests because those things help determine what the Cathedral is going to be. Likewise, I deal with a bishop only to the degree that he has effected important changes in the Cathedral itself or its programs, and not every bishop has been inclined to do that.

One of the happy tasks any author gets to perform is acknowledging those who have helped him bring the book to completion. Pride of place among my acknowledgments must go to Cathedral rector Monsignor Joseph M. Mayo, who first broached the idea that I might undertake such a project. My supervisors at the Diocesan Pastoral Center, Chancellor Deacon Silvio Mayo and Vicar General Msgr. J. Terrence Fitzgerald, have supported me fully and allowed me to undertake this book as part of my regular work load. Bishop John C. Wester also supported the project and graciously agreed to write the foreword.

When I began the project, my intention was to have it published by an academic press which, through its peer review process, would lend credibility to the quality of scholarship in the book. However, since I began the book at a late date and felt myself under some pressure to get it into print at least roughly coinciding with August 15, 2009, the centennial anniversary of the Cathedral, I was unable to wait for the slow wheels of academic bureaucracy to grind to their conclusion, so I asked Ann Torrence to issue it as an imprint of her Sagebrush Press. I am most grateful for the quality of her work. At the same time, in order to approximate the academic peer review process, I asked several experts to read parts or the whole of the manuscript. Thus I am grateful to Msgr. J. Terrence Fitzgerald, Msgr. Joseph M. Mayo, Msgr. M. Francis Mannion, and historian-editor Robert J. Welsh for their critical suggestions. Msgr. Mannion and Madeleine Choir School founder Gregory Glenn sat for extensive interviews regarding their roles in the renovation of the 1990s. It is my belief that the contributions of those persons have given the book a scholarly credibility equal to that of academic press books.

My own research has been significantly supplemented by the work of a group of Cathedral aficionados who made this project more fun than I could ever have expected. Laurel Dokos-Griffith, Cathedral Development Director, has prompted our research on various historical themes for the annual Bishop's Dinner. Researcher extraordinaire Isaac Goeckeritz led the research team for those dinners. Cathedral tour guide Lyle Bate discussed Cathedral minutiae with me on many occasions in addition to counting—and verifying by recount—the 258 angels that exist in the Cathedral! Art historian Marty Seiner joined me in a futile (to this date, at least) search for the whereabouts of the five Sorrowful Mystery windows removed from the apse during Bishop Glass's renovation. Laurel, Marty, and I also collaborated on an exhibit of historic Cathedral photographs to celebrate the centennial.

Finally, my interest and research in Cathedral history has been inspired and guided for some three decades by my great predecessor as diocesan archivist, Bernice Maher Mooney. Her long life at the Cathedral has been deeply steeped in the traditions, the lore, and the personalities of that great edifice. Extensive passages of her prose ennoble my own text. This book is dedicated to her.

Gary Topping

When Gary Topping asked me to make new photographs of the Cathedral of the Madeleine to accompany his book, I declined. I am not an architectural photographer and many excellent photographs exist of the building, made as the latest renovation was completed. But, as Bernice Maher Mooney insisted that Gary write, so he insisted I photograph.

Without a congregation, a cathedral is little more than a museum. I hope my photographs show a portrait of the community of faith that calls the Cathedral of the Madeleine its home. I am grateful to the many people who graciously helped me to make these images: Bishop John C. Wester, Msgr. Joseph M. Mayo, Deacon Silvio Mayo, Deacon Scott Dodge, Deacon Lynn Johnson, Willie Green, Arlita Llenares, Kent Lowe, Douglas O'Neill and Darren Williams.

Ann Torrence

Fig. 6: Original Cathedral interior.

Chapter 1

Creation

"And God saw that it was good." (Genesis 1:31)

The origins of Catholicism in Utah date back to the first thrust of Spanish explorers into the American Southwest during the Coronado expedition of 1540–42. The first Catholics actually to enter the modern area of Utah were military spies masquerading as traders sent north into the Ute country from Santa Fe under the leadership of Juan Maria Antonio de Rivera in two expeditions in the spring and fall of 1765. In 1776, even as the Declaration of Independence was being signed at the other end of the continent, the celebrated expedition under the Franciscan friars Dominguez and Escalante was crossing Utah in quest of a land route linking Santa Fe with the California missions. During the early nineteenth century, fur trappers moving north from Taos, New Mexico, west from St. Louis, Missouri, and south from Canada explored the Rocky Mountains and the Great Basin; some of them, like Etienne Provot, Kit Carson, and Denis Julien, were Catholics.[1]

A few priests began to venture into the region at midcentury and to lay the foundations for what Msgr. Jerome Stoffel called "the hesitant beginnings of the Catholic Church in Utah." In the summer of 1859 Father Bonaventure Keller, a Conventual Franciscan in the customary black robe of his order, paused to minister to the Catholic soldiers of Camp Floyd for a period of about six months. He offered Mass, performed baptisms, marriages, and funerals for Catholics who were either soldiers, teamsters, or suppliers who accompanied the federal troops who were sent to Utah in 1857–58.

Fig. 7: Bishop Lawrence Scanlan, first Bishop of the Diocese of Salt Lake.

Five years later, Father John Batiste Raverdy came to serve the Irish soldiers under General Patrick E. Connor at Fort Douglas, offering in 1864 the first known Mass within the present confines of the Cathedral parish.[2]

The first permanent Catholic presence in Utah came in the form of Father Edward Kelly, who was sent to Salt Lake City in 1866 by Archbishop Joseph Sadoc Alemany of San Francisco. On November 6 of that year, Kelly purchased a small adobe building and a lot on the west side of Second East between South Temple and First South. Kelly was apparently assisted in the purchase by the Catholic people of the city, who bonded themselves $2,899, a sum which included funds to enlarge the building, which Father Kelly intended to use as a school as well as a church. Unfortunately, Kelly learned that the title to the property was flawed, and the resolution of the matter involved the first contact between the Catholic church and The Church of Jesus Christ of Latter-day Saints (LDS). Kelly asserted that "he wanted no legal proceedings; that he bought the property in good faith, and had paid the market price for it," according to Father Denis Kiely, who wrote the first history of the diocese in 1900. Kelly and his opponent agreed to submit the matter to Brigham Young for arbitration, and the LDS president ruled in favor the Catholic.[3]

Although Father Kelly was recalled to California before he could establish much of a ministry in Salt Lake City, from the small adobe structure on that property—the first Catholic church in Utah—his successor Father James Foley ministered to the few Catholic families from January or February 1870 to July 1871. Among those laypersons were Cornelia Bibb Vaughan, wife of Territorial Governor Vernon H. Vaughan, and the wife and children of Territorial Judge Thomas Marshall. In 1871 Archbishop Alemany then assigned Father Patrick Walsh to continue the work begun in Salt Lake City. Father Walsh saw promise for the Church in Utah and on the site of the small adobe building constructed the precursor of the present Cathedral, "a typical carpenter's Gothic structure of yellow brick surmounted by a belfry," as the *Salt Lake Tribune* called it[4]. Archbishop Alemany himself came to dedicate it under the enduring patronage of St. Mary Magdalene in November 1871.[5]

In 1873 Father Walsh asked to return to Amador County, California, from which he had come. In his search for a replacement, Archbishop Alemany had to find someone of great zeal and resourcefulness who could forge a solid Catholic presence out of a sparse Catholic population with limited financial means. Such a person would have to be a man of great physical strength and capable of enduring considerable privations as he ministered throughout what would become the geographically largest diocese in the country.[6] It would be very hard to ascribe to anything but Divine Providence his choice of the young Irish priest, Father Lawrence Scanlan, a man who embodied those qualities to exponential degrees, whose name will forever be synonymous with the Diocese of Salt Lake City, and who, as first bishop of the diocese, was appropriately interred in a sarcophagus in the basement of his great Cathedral of the Madeleine.

Lawrence Scanlan entered the world on September 28, 1843 as the firstborn of an Irish farm family of apparently modest prosperity near the village of Ballytarsna in the parish of Moyne, Cashel County, near the 12th century Cistercian monastery, Holy Cross Abbey. The church loomed over the boy spiritually as well as physically, for legend has it that his parents dedicated him to be a missionary priest and even foresaw his destiny as a Prince of the Church — not an unusual thing for a pious Irish family to do, though hindsight has a way of coloring such memories.[7] Although the Scanlan farm was about one hundred acres in size and situated in a fertile region of the country, "the area he was raised in," a family descendant reported, "was always noted for its hard-working people … so I can guess that the young Lawrence was no stranger to toil." If so, those labors hardened his already powerful physique, for his biographer records that he was reputedly the "greatest athlete" at his seminary: "He excelled, it seems, in all the sports, jumping higher, throwing farther, kicking more accurately than any of his companions in the cassock. Certainly he had the build for it, this six-footer with his mop of black hair, his vast shoulders, and his comfortably large feet and hands."

After completing his preparatory studies in Classics, the future bishop entered All Hallows Seminary in Dublin. It was the most rigorous and yet the most appropriate training a potential missionary priest could have experienced. Founded the year before Scanlan's birth by "a zealous priest," Father John Hand, the seminary was designed to train priests who would minister to Irish expatriates of the Potato Famine in their diaspora throughout the world. Its faculty, "as devoted a group of priests as ever staffed a school," taught by example as well as precept, for Father Hand asked them "to accept no salary and to live in poverty equal to that which would confront the priest on the mission in his most difficult assignment."

It was while at All Hallows that Father Scanlan's future was revealed to him, for both students and faculty had been set afire by a visit in 1850 from the young California archbishop, Joseph Sadoc Alemany, who inspired faculty and students to dedicate their lives to ministering to Irish Catholics in the frontier gold mining towns of the Far West, and the zeal he had ignited was still burning brightly when Father Scanlan graduated and was ordained on June 28, 1868. Al-

Fig. 8: Father Lawrence Scanlan at about the time he arrived in the United States (1869).

most immediately he embarked for America, and he never saw the green hills of Ireland again. Upon his arrival in San Francisco, the young priest was briefly assigned to Old St. Patrick's Church on Mission Street, but he soon found himself dispatched to the Diocese of Marysville, where Bishop Eugene O'Connell, himself a graduate of All Hallows, was seeking priests to minister in the Wild West mining camps of Nevada, and he assigned Father Scanlan to the community of Pioche.

After surviving the boot camp of All Hallows, Father Scanlan was under no illusions of a life of luxury in Pioche. In fact, even getting there taxed his stamina. The Central Pacific Railroad could take him only part way; he had to travel by primitive stage nearly three hundred miles south to his new post. Lying over at Hamilton to rest along the way, Father Scanlan fell ill with what was later diagnosed as a severe case of "mountain fever" (perhaps Lyme's disease, which is spread by ticks) lasting some weeks. "There is evidence," his biographer reports, "that the effects of this sickness were lifelong, contributing in no small measure to the exhaustion and debility of his later years."[8]

When Father Scanlan at last rode into Pioche, he was yet a few months short of his twenty-sixth birthday. Pioche was, in Father Dwyer's words, "one of the toughest and wildest of the fabulous Nevada camps," and his

Fig. 9: Nora Gleason, Cathedral organist and choir director under Bishop Scanlan.

nearest fellow priest was some one hundred miles away, though with the primitive transportation of the day, it "might just as well have been a thousand."[9] It was rough duty, and one might reasonably speculate that some of the feelings and forces he was subject to then contributed in later years to his occasional severity with his own young priests.

His countrymen initially welcomed him and helped him erect a frame church (dedicated to St. Lawrence, of course) with rooms for himself in the rear. But the warmth turned to chill when he learned of their dissolute recreational pursuits in the barroom and the house of ill repute and began preaching against them. "As contributions fell off," Father Dwyer says, "he visited the Chinese restaurant at rarer intervals, grew more gaunt than ever, and his clothes took on the color of the Nevada sand. But the sermons kept hitting home, and the lines of his face hardened."[10] As he persevered, though, he gradually won them over in what ended in a successful apostolate that proved the young priest's missionary mettle to Archbishop Alemany. When Father Walsh asked to be transferred from Salt Lake City back to California, the archbishop had a replacement ready at hand, one who had proved himself under the heat of the western sun.

When Father Scanlan entered Salt Lake City on August 14, 1873, at long last the Catholic Church had come to stay. The mission included the entire Territory of Utah. Father Scanlan could not foresee, as he got his bearings there, that within some eighteen years Pope Leo XIII would elevate the Church of Utah to the status of a diocese. By 1909 Catholics there would number 10,000, and the diocese, embracing 153,768 square miles (82,190 in Utah and 71,578 in Nevada), would be the largest in the United States. The Archdiocese of New York City, by comparison, with Archbishop Farley and seven suffragan bishops, encompassed only 55,376 square miles, or less than one-third the size of Salt Lake.

With his characteristic vision and determination, Father Scanlan set about getting to know his flock of some ninety Catholics in Salt Lake City and Ogden combined, and some 710 others dispersed along railroad divisions and in mining camps and villages throughout the territory. He moved into rooms in the back of St. Mary's church, built in 1871 to replace the original adobe structure used for the first Catholic church from 1870 to 1871. It is believed his rooms were connected with the apse of the church; other rooms were added in 1877.

Father Scanlan lived in this building with only the bare necessities of life. "The privations which surrounded him," observes one historian, "gave zest and energy to his missionary spirit."[11] Father Lawrence Breslin was his assistant for about a year, but in 1874 he was joined by Father Denis Kiely, the priest whose career was to be associated with his own over the next forty years. From 1874 to 1915 their companionship was interrupted only by the missionary travels of one or the other. Born in Waterford, Ireland, Father Kiely, too, had set sail for America shortly after his ordination. He proved an indefatigable worker in Utah and collected much of the funds for the construction of the present-day Cathedral. His biography, written into the heart of the Cathedral, parallels that of the man to whom he was friend, companion, assistant pastor, rector, Chancellor and Vicar General over nearly half a century.

The two of them traveled a circuit by carriage or stagecoach at least monthly from Park City to Bingham Canyon, Mercur, Stockton and Ophir. The people who flowed into Utah to work those mines and the wealth they produced made possible the development of the Church in Utah. As the fortunes of people like Thomas Kearns, John J. Daly, and John and Mary Judge changed from poverty to wealth, their mansions slowly rose up along South Temple and other elegant districts. Some of their signatures remain beneath stained-glass windows they donated to the Cathedral.

But lesser known figures made their mark on Cathedral history and legend as well. One was the eccentric musical genius Nora Gleason, whose parents were Potato Famine exiles from Ireland who migrated to the mines of southern Nevada and Utah in the 1870s. They reportedly met Father Scanlan on his visits to establish a church, school, and hospital in Silver Reef. Apparently impressed with young Nora's talents on the piano and

Fig. 10: St. Mary's Church, Second East between South Temple and First South. This church functioned as Salt Lake City's first cathedral.

organ, Father Scanlan brought her to Salt Lake City to pursue her education at St. Mary's Academy and then he evidently raised money for further musical training in Chicago. Miss Gleason never married, and devoted her life to directing the musical program at St. Mary's church and later the Cathedral, while supporting herself in part by giving private lessons on piano, organ, mandolin and guitar. She died in 1918 at age forty-five, surviving her beloved bishop by only three years.

Constant appeals to his people, both rich and poor, enabled Father Scanlan to clear the $6,000 debt on St. Mary Magdalene's within two years after his arrival. His tall, imposing figure, like "a sort of ecclesiastical John Wayne,"[12] hovered around the entrances to the mines on payday. He established a miners' pension fund promising any miner who contributed to the fund would be given free care by the Sisters at their hospital in case of illness. He was loved by the miners in the camps he visited and was not afraid to go down among them into the shafts. He had an excellent command of the German language, learned for the purpose of serving those who spoke only that tongue. What could be called a financial prowess was abetted by the personal charisma of the friendly man with the diplomatic manner, and was responsible for the construction of all the Catholic parishes and charitable and educational institutions in Utah over the next forty years. He worked for a widespread parish school system and a proliferation of Catholic lay organizations.

But, especially at first, financial support was hard to come by and it was only the deep interior faith of the genuinely holy Father Scanlan that enabled his survival. There was some limited financial assistance from outside the territory. One was an organization of French lay people, the Society for the Propagation of the Faith, which helped support struggling Catholic foundations like Utah. For a time in the late 1870s the Society made annual contributions in response to appeals from needy regions, totaling $16,400 for the Metropolitan Province of San Francisco between 1872 and 1887. Out of that, Father Scanlan reported receiving $1,560 in 1875, perhaps a typical annual sum.[13]

By now the Catholic population under Father Scanlan's care numbered nearly 5,000 people, its largest parish being the flourishing St. Mary of the Assumption in Park City with a membership of 800, while Salt Lake City now had 400. With that kind of growth, it seems almost inevitable that steps would be taken toward creation of a new diocese. In 1886 Father Scanlan was named Titular Bishop of Larandum and Vicar Apostolic of Utah. Despite the alleged prophecies surrounding his birth, it was an unexpected development for the frontier priest for whom, as Father Kiely put it, "the simple garb of pastor was preferable to the episcopal ermine," and in fact the new bishop learned of his appointment from a *Salt Lake Tribune* reporter.[14] No doubt foreseeing the greater challenges that would accompany his elevation to the episcopacy, he chose a motto that would strengthen his courage — *Quid Timidi Estis?* (What Do You Fear?) — though the plural verb indicates his prayer that all Catholics in the new vicariate would be emboldened as well.

Elevation of Utah to a vicariate suggested that plans for a new cathedral would not be inappropriate. Old St. Mary's, although a majestic yellow brick structure that towered above its neighbors, had been designed for a Catholic population of barely two dozen people, and had already become inadequate. On February 25, 1890, supported by the new silver wealth within the Catholic community, Bishop Scanlan purchased Lot 2, Block 12, Plat D in Salt Lake City, the property on which the Cathedral of the Madeleine and the rectory now stand, from Sarah M. McKibben for $35,000. On March 24, Lot 3, where the north parking lot is now located, was purchased from Lorenzo D. Young for $14,500 by warranty deed.[15] Confirmation of the wisdom of the purchase came in 1891 when the Vicariate Apostolate was constituted a diocese and Bishop Scanlan fixed his cathedral throne in Salt Lake City. He completed a rectory on the new site and moved into it within the year.[16]

Now specific plans could be formulated. The new Cathedral would be spiritually akin to the ancient one of Bishop Scanlan's ordination in Ireland and to that of his consecration in St. Mary's Cathedral in San Francisco. As in the great churches of Europe, the Gothic architecture would write its own image of infinity, its spires drawing man's heart and thoughts upwards toward God, while the spacious interior would be lit through stained glass windows proclaiming the Gospel and symbolizing the light of Truth. Scanlan's Cathedral would retain that quality of ancient times when the majesty of the mother church of the diocese towered over lesser secular buildings, its solid stone structure reminding one of eternity. It would unite the once-isolated territory with its fellow pioneer missions throughout the West — Boise, Helena, Cheyenne, and Denver — symbolizing its attachment to the Archdiocese of San Francisco and, beyond that, to the Holy See itself.

In Salt Lake City, it would express the abiding presence of Catholicism in the valley, standing as it would almost in the shadow of the massive

Mormon Temple being completed on the spot Brigham Young had designated in 1847. The differences in the size of the two buildings, their architecture, their location—one in the center of town, the other slightly to the side—somehow blend in a remarkable juxtaposition of two cultures and beliefs. Both grew out of the milieu of frontier America. Though irreconcilable in theologies and institutional underpinnings, both communities were nevertheless united in their official stance of toleration for each other and a sense of mutual compassion for a world in need of Christian love.

One must admit, however, that it was surely a tenuous harmony within this apparently peaceful coexistence because the beliefs of Catholics and Mormons are so basically opposed. There remained an uneasy undercurrent of subsurface sectarianism, though when the subconscious hostility surfaced it was often private. For example, "while it cannot be said that Bishop Scanlan was silent on the subject of polygamy," his biographer reports, "it is evident that he confined his remarks to his own pulpit in moral discourses to his own people, and chose rather to cultivate amicable relations with individual Mormons, some of whom [as late as 1940] still recall his friendly spirit toward them during the periods of sharpest antagonism." Although "he came to Utah too late to know Brigham Young in the latter's prime, ... years later, at the unveiling of the famous monument to the great colonizer and leader, he referred with no little feeling to Young's personal benevolence toward him and his fellow Catholics in the days when the Church was struggling to obtain a footing in Utah."[17]

There were by now some 5,000 Catholics in the diocese. They were a people of diverse origins. In the future, when their Cathedral would become a reality, many of their entire life spans would be lived out in the shades of its towers. The great church would channel their heritage of faith from one generation to another. Take, for example, the Gorlinski family: Robert Gorlinski had studied voice in Europe and Father Scanlan took him to San Francisco to be the soloist at his consecration ceremonies. The Gorlinski family remained an integral part of Cathedral life through many years, especially in the person of Robert's daughter, Valentine. Well-versed in the history of both architecture and of Christianity, for years she conducted tours of the Cathedral oriented toward illustrating how everything in the building relates to Christ's life and teachings.

Likewise, the family of Decker Little seems to incorporate the entire history of the Cathedral. Symbolic of the intermingling of the forces of Mormonism and Catholicism in Salt Lake Valley, Decker Little was a direct descendant of John Young, Brigham Young's father. Although his mother, Alice Soule, had been baptized Catholic as an infant in France, she was brought to Utah in 1863 by relatives who had converted to Mormonism. One of her uncles filed a mining claim for her in Bingham Canyon which became productive and she was able to take care of her mother and sisters, as well as put herself through a Catholic girls' school in Oakland, California. Eventually she married James T. Little, cashier of Deseret National Bank, with whom she had three sons and five daughters. One of their granddaughters joined the Holy Cross Sisters, while their son Decker worked on the renovation of the interior of the Cathedral under Bishop Joseph S. Glass. He attended church at the old St. Mary's and was confirmed by the then-aging Bishop Scanlan. His whole life was a commentary on interfaith relations on the Utah frontier.[18]

Positioned in the midst of the Mormon metropolis, the Cathedral would reconcile Catholicism to the community and to the West. Bishop Scanlan drew the final plans for the structure over a period of eight years from the time of the purchase of the site. The groundbreaking took place on Independence Day 1899, and the cornerstone was laid barely a year later, on July 22, 1900.

The original plan called for a sandstone structure unadorned by towers, with interior brick lining placed on a granite foundation—in other words, not too different in appearance from the previous cathedral. The design would be the Romanesque style then popular in America. "The building will add much to the beauty of Salt Lake ... and stand as a monument to the piety and liberality of some of the best people of our city," the *Salt Lake Mining Review* exulted. "The structure will cover a ground space of 99 x 185' and will be built of gray Kyune stone. The interior will be in keeping with the elegance of the exterior, the building to be illuminated by 1,500 electric lights."[19]

Funds for the work were partially assured through the Pious Fund of the Californias from which, by 1890, the Archbishop of San Francisco had distributed annual subsidies of some $68,494 to the Utah territory. The Pious Fund had been established in 1697 by the Society of Jesus for the work of evangelizing Lower California and Arizona. In a confusing history, it was administered by the Society until the expulsion of the Jesuits from the New World in 1767, after which the Spanish crown controlled it until the Mexican government took it over following the Revolution of 1821. The Bishop of the Diocese of the Californias controlled it from 1836 until 1842 when General Antonio Lopez de Santa Anna confiscated the funds. The flow of money ceased completely at the end of the Mexican War of 1846–48. Political and legal maneuvering followed, which eventually brought the matter before an international tribunal at The Hague, which required Mexico to reimburse the Bishops of California for payments in arrears plus interest. Eventually the Diocese of Salt Lake City received $124,080 from the Pious Fund, the greater portion of which Bishop Scanlan used for the building of the Cathedral. In 1912 the Mexican government, more preoccupied with revolution than with Catholic missions, defaulted permanently on its Pious Fund payments. By 1904 Bishop Scanlan had collected another $87,579 from Catholics of Utah and Nevada. The final report Bishop Scanlan filed in 1912, after the financial dust had settled on the overall project, indicated totals of just over $300,000 spent on construction and almost $44,000 on furnishings.[20]

Carl M. Neuhausen was chosen as the architect. Born in Germany in 1853, he was educated in Stuttgart and shortly afterwards came to America, settling in Minneapolis. His architectural studies took him throughout the United States and Canada before he moved to Salt Lake City in 1892. From his office in the Dooley Building on South Temple at B Street, right across the street from the Cathedral, Neuhausen designed some of the city's most monumental structures, including the Saltair pavilion, the Kearns mansion, the D. F. Walker Block, St. Ann's Orphanage, and the chapel at Holy Cross Hospital, in addition to the Cathedral.

Although Neuhausen did not live to see the completion of the Cathedral, it was he who established its general shape. The style expanded from pure Romanesque into what is known as Transition, a mixture of Gothic (the façade and much of the interior) and Romanesque (the sides and rear). Advancements in engineering and materials had done away with the need for the flying buttresses used in the medieval churches. Neuhausen was likely influenced as well by examples of Rhenish architecture in his native Germany.

Fig. 11: Cathedral under construction.

From 1899 to 1907 construction went forward at a leisurely pace, mostly because Bishop Scanlan preferred to pay for the work as it went along rather than to accomplish a faster progress at the expense of accumulated debt. "There is evidence that Neuhausen revamped his blueprints from time to time as work progressed," Scanlan's biographer observes, "adding towers as additional funds justified the expense and in general adapting his progress to fit the ecclesiastical purse."[21] Neuhausen's death in 1907 delayed the work which, nevertheless, received new impetus at this time by handsome donations from individual Catholics.

Architect Bernard R. Mecklenburg was hired to finish the Norman towers and roof. The clerestory planned by Neuhausen was eliminated and all three aisles covered under a single roof, an unusual and distinguishing feature of the structure. When finally the main portion of the building was completed, the Bishop postponed decoration of the interior and completion of the steeples in favor of fitting up the basement auditorium as a place where Mass might be offered until funds were available for completion of the upper levels. Chromolith stations and kerosene lamps faded into memory as the old St. Mary's was stripped of its religious furnishings and its doors closed after the last Mass on December 27, 1907. The building stood until 1918 when the property was sold and commercial development in the area necessitated its destruction.

It is difficult to imagine the effect the spectacle of the medieval stone building under construction in the midst of Salt Lake City might have had on observers, though perhaps their awe had been blunted a bit after having witnessed the construction of the city's other monumental ecclesiastical structure, the Mormon temple. For years the cathedral block on South Temple resembled a rock quarry more than a church site. A crane swung the huge stones upward to ever more vertigo-inducing heights, where they were transported to their proper place by carts on a railroad track.

By 1909 the new Cathedral stood substantially as it is today except for the decoration of the interior, which was a plain plaster finish. As Bishop Scanlan's personal energies waned and his funds ebbed, he simply painted it, like his old St. Mary's, green for the walls and white for the pillars. Attention focused now on interior furnishings and excitement mounted as, one by one, they were put in place. Generally they were in accordance with the prevalent artistic taste of the time. Making no claim to be an artist himself, Bishop Scanlan did prefer the popular Carrara marble for the altar, feeling that the pure white marble of the old St. Mary's did not fit into the overall unity of effect in the new building. It is said that representatives hunted throughout the region around the Italian city of Carrara itself but could not locate a suitable type of stone. In some discouragement, the search was resumed in Utah and the desired marble (with brown mottled effect) was found in the central part of the state. The *Intermountain Catholic* announced that the altars were installed in December, 1908.[22]

Fig. 12: Dedication of the Cathedral, August 15, 1909.

The stained glass windows, which depict the Joyful Mysteries of the Rosary on the west side, the Sorrowful Mysteries in the apse (later removed) and the Glorious Mysteries on the east, were designed by Francis X. Zettler of the House of Littler in the Royal Bavarian Institute in Neuhausen's native Germany. At least two of the windows in ends of the transept were arranged for in Europe by Mrs. Mary Judge, who dedicated them to the memory of her husband, the mining magnate John Judge, and her relatives. Others were donated by various patrons like Father Kiely, who dedicated the Assumption window to his mother and father; the miner Patrick Phelan, whose fortune dedicated in part to the support of orphans, was tapped for the Annunciation window; and a Nevadan, Miss Ellen Hayes, whose mining fortune paid for two windows. At Bishop Scanlan's insistence, the style of the windows was realism, for he wanted them to be didactic as well as aesthetic. Although that realistic style had fallen out of favor in Catholic art as early as the time of Scanlan's successor, Bishop Joseph S. Glass, the windows are one of the Cathedral's distinctive and memorable features.[23]

By February 1909 the doors, two confessionals and the bishop's throne had arrived. By summer the pews, windows, and organ had been installed. On August 7, 1909, the *Intermountain Catholic* warned that rental seats for the dedication service the following week were going fast, to applicants from Nevada, Wyoming and Idaho as well as Utah, at the steep rates of $25, $17.50 and $12.50 for family pews and $5 for single seats. In order that poor people could participate in the dedication of their cathedral, though, Bishop Scanlan reserved a block of seats at $1 and $2.[24]

Bishop Scanlan had had some experience with these ceremonies. In 1906 he had journeyed to Boise for the laying of the cornerstone of its new cathedral, which he described as the exact model of his St. Mary's with only a slight difference in height. A year later he had traveled to Omaha for the laying of the cornerstone of its cathedral by his dear friend Bishop James O'Connor, and in February he had sent his felicitations upon the dedication of the cathedral in Cheyenne. Now, he would summon his failing strength to celebrate the pontifical Mass dedicating his own Cathedral of St. Mary Magdalene.

As a prelude to the ceremonies, Dean W. R. Harris accompanied him to Pocatello to meet James Cardinal Gibbons, who had been visiting national parks on his way to Utah for the dedication. Harris had hurriedly finished his history of *The Catholic Church in Utah, 1776–1909* in order to present it to Bishop Scanlan the morning of the cathedral dedication.[25] The dedication ceremony presided over by Cardinal Gibbons on August 15, 1909 proved to be "one of the most brilliant assemblies of American Church dignitaries the Far West had ever seen," with bishops and archbishops attending from as far away as Omaha, Dubuque, and St. Louis.[26] Mixed choirs under the direction of Nora Gleason, who also played the new organ, dignified the ceremony, which was also commemorated by the issue of special lapel buttons and a small brochure of photographs. Evidence of the pressures under which construction workers had been working is the fact that the ambo (pulpit) had not yet been installed in its permanent location east of the sanctuary, but instead was placed in the middle of the aisle just outside the altar rail.[27]

The celebration climaxed Bishop Scanlan's work and, though only sixty-six years old at the time, his strength was waning and, as his biographer notes, he began more and more to assume "the role of a passive spectator."

Physical problems incurred during his rough years as a missionary priest began to assert themselves, not only from the mountain fever he had contracted, but also from a head injury in a fall from a horse that caused him severe pain. Although he never retired and resisted efforts to send him an Auxiliary Bishop, at the age of seventy he left the rectory and moved into quarters at Holy Cross Hospital.[28]

Even though he had remained with them long past his prime his contemporaries still venerated the singular greatness of the man. One of the Apostles of the LDS church commented, "I regard Bishop Scanlan as being the finest character of the present century. I consider him a saintly man who has won the sincere love and respect of every man and woman in the state of Utah by the true godliness of his life."[29] To the Catholic community he was a figure of Old Testament grandeur who had helped the Lord gather a people unto himself. Throughout the territory men and women whose lives he had touched held their own private memories of their hard-working leader. James Ivers, Jr., recalled driving one day with his father in a buggy along South Temple past the present site of the Holy Cross Hospital. They noticed a man plowing in the field and his father drove the buggy over by the plowman who engaged in friendly conversation with them. As they bade farewell and drove away, James, Sr. said to his son, "Do you know who he is? Did you see the ring on his finger? That is Bishop Scanlan."

That same ring figured in the Bishop's last hours. He had been confined to bed and on May 10, 1915 interrupted Father Kiely nearby, lifting his finger for his episcopal ring. That ring had been worn for three centuries by the Bishops of Cashel in Ireland. Archbishop Croke had given it to Bishop Scanlan as a young man still in school, predicting that it would be his episcopal ring as a bishop in America. Feeling it slipped on now by his faithful old friend, he became content to die, and slipped away to his eternal reward.

Two days later his remains were taken from the funeral parlor in solemn procession to the Cathedral, where they lay in state until the funeral on May 14. Archbishop Edward Hanna of San Francisco, in his funeral oration, said, "The secret of a man's inspiration is hidden in his heart. If we study the life of Bishop Scanlan we can discover the secret of his inspiration — the life of Christ was one of sacrifice, and so was his."[30]

At the dedication of the cathedral six years earlier, Cardinal Gibbons had suggested that Bishop Scanlan's final resting place should be in that very cathedral, the monumental symbol of his ministry in Utah. Thus it was that, in accordance with his own last request, he was interred in a crypt within the Cathedral. The crypt, a vault in which traditionally saints and martyrs are buried, was not open for public viewing as are some in Europe. In the small narrow room there stood the marble sarcophagus which enclosed the wooden coffin. There was a glass window through which were visible the coffin and a nameplate with the Latin inscription reading, "Reverend Lawrence Scanlan, D.D., First Bishop of Salt Lake; born A.D. 1843; consecrated 1887; died May 10, 1915. Rest in Peace."

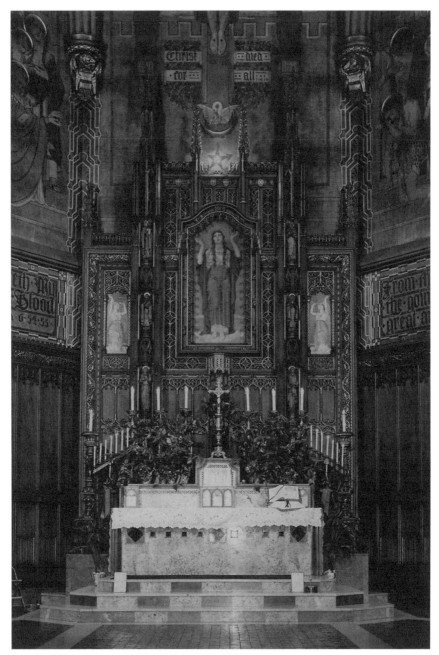

Fig. 13: High altar installed by Bishop Glass.

Chapter 2

Transformation

"Behold, I make all things new." (Revelation 21:5)

The last three years of Bishop Scanlan's life (1912–15) were a tough time for him and for the diocese. One problem, as noted in the previous chapter, was the bishop's physical deterioration, which caused him to spend lengthy periods at a hot springs in Arizona seeking relief from pain. At the same time, Father Kiely, his Vicar General, was losing his eyesight and his mental acuity, thus diminishing the effectiveness of his leadership in the bishop's absence.[1] The result was a diocese ridden with conflict and apparently bereft of leadership. On a trip to Salt Lake City, San Francisco Archbishop Patrick Riordan told Bishop Scanlan that he was going to ask Rome to appoint a coadjutor bishop with right of succession. Unwilling effectively to surrender control of the diocese with which he had been so integrally associated, Bishop Scanlan initially refused to accept anything but an auxiliary bishop, but eventually accepted an auxiliary who would also be Vicar General, which would mean essentially the same thing as a coadjutor. Ultimately it became a moot point, because Bishop Scanlan died before such an appointment could be made.[2]

His successor, Bishop Joseph Sarsfield Glass, C.M., was about the greatest contrast to Bishop Scanlan one could imagine. Rather than the ascetic Irish missionary hardened on the western frontier, Bishop Glass had been born to affluence and was accustomed to moving in the high society of Los Angeles. Where Bishop Scanlan had been frugal and insisted upon

Fig. 14: Bishop Joseph S. Glass on the day of his ordination in Los Angeles, California.

paying his bills as he went along, Bishop Glass was impatient with delayed gratification and spent far ahead of his resources. Where Bishop Scanlan was the humble priest who could be seen plowing a field and who was careless of his dress and appearance, Bishop Glass was an old-fashioned Prince of the Church accustomed to the comforts and trappings of authority. The Diocese of Salt Lake was in for some interesting times.

Joseph Glass was born March 13, 1874 in Bushnell, Illinois, to a wholesale liquor dealer, James Glass, who had converted to Catholicism from Protestantism when he married his second wife, Mary Kelley. His lifelong affiliation with California began in 1887 when the family moved to Pasadena in the interest of his mother's health. The move was of little benefit to her, however, and she died later that year. Another important connection occurred in California, when his father enrolled him in St. Vincent's College in Los Angeles run by the Congregation of the Mission, or the Vincentian order, which he himself joined in 1891. (To date, Bishop Glass is the only bishop of the Diocese of Salt Lake City to have been a member of a religious order.) After studies at Saint Mary's Seminary in Perryville, Missouri, he was ordained in 1897. Graduate studies in theology in Rome led to a doctorate in 1899 and appointment as a professor of moral theology at his old seminary. In 1901 he returned to Los Angeles as president of St. Vincent's College. It was a lofty position, as his biographer points out, for a twenty-seven-year-old who had been a priest for only four years, and it speaks highly of his precocious abilities.[3]

It may also have meant that he was biting off more than he could chew, for the college was at a point of crisis. Educational developments in Los Angeles indicated a need for expansion at St. Vincent's, both in size and in diversity of curriculum, and Bishop Thomas Conaty of Los Angeles was putting pressure on the Vincentians to accomplish that expansion. The Vincentians, however, including Father Glass, argued that the apostolate of the Congregation of the Mission was not education, but rather parish missions, and that the order should turn the college over to the Jesuits. When the Jesuits indicated a lack of interest in the school, Father Glass simply closed it. The closing left the Vincentians with a great deal of debt, for the college had been indebted when Glass took it over, and the red ink had flowed even more freely during his administration. "Accusations of conduct that bordered on the criminal were made against him," his biographer notes. It was the first, but not the last, indication that "at best he had an elastic conscience in matters of money."[4]

Fortunately he made another contact during this time who would provide a financial shock absorber during the rest of his life. Father Glass was pastor of St. Vincent's church in Los Angeles, and almost certainly its wealthiest parishioner was the oil magnate Edward L. Doheny.[5] Despite his grandfatherly appearance, Doheny was a ruthless Robber Baron not at all unlike his eastern counterpart, John D. Rockefeller. In his oil exploitation in Mexico, he had nearly gotten the United States into war with that country; he had helped the hapless Warren G. Harding gain the Presidency so that he and other oilmen could exploit the country's richest oil reserves without the necessity of competitive bidding; and, though he was never convicted, he bribed Interior Secretary Albert B. Fall for the exclusive drilling rights to the Elk Hills reserve in southern California. Despite his legal and ethical fluidity, Doheny was a devoted Catholic who virtually adopted the young Glass into his household. Glass returned the favor by securing an annulment for Doheny so he could marry a second time to Carrie Estelle Betzold, and then baptized her into the church. To be fair, Father Glass was never implicated in any of Doheny's dubious dealings, though funds from the Doheny fortune were greatly beneficial to the Vincentians in California and later to Bishop Glass in Salt Lake City. Bishop Glass, indeed, was a churchman not a businessman, and because Doheny in fact never was convicted of a crime, the bishop seems to have been unaware of the true nature of his patron's business practices.

Bishop Glass received episcopal ordination at St. Vincent's on August 24, 1915, a scant three months after his predecessor's death, and was installed at the Cathedral of the Madeleine on September 1. He liked little of what he found in Salt Lake City. For one thing, the Cathedral rectory had fallen into an appalling condition during the years of Bishop Scanlan's infirmity. Although Bishop Glass spent a good deal of his money from ordination gifts on its renovation, he lived there only briefly until he could purchase his own home, at 82 Laurel Avenue, for which he spent $25,000 of his own money. The Dohenys furnished the house so that their favorite priest, now bishop, could live in the style to which he had been accustomed. They also gave him a monthly stipend of $750, most of which he passed on to his priests, and two Pierce Arrow automobiles. One of the cars he gave to the sisters at Holy Cross Hospital, and the other he retained for his personal use, though despite driving lessons, he never learned to operate it himself.[6]

The other thing he disliked was the Cathedral itself, for he thought the realistic style of the stained glass windows was out of fashion, and he deemed Bishop Scanlan's simple green and white paint scheme too modest. On the latter point Bishop Scanlan might have agreed, for he had been tired and out of funds as the Cathedral neared completion, and may have regarded the simple decoration as an expedient to get the church functioning and dedicated. In any event, Bishop Glass, who had a longtime interest in art and architecture and even experience in church renovation at St. Vincent's in Los Angeles, was well qualified to paint upon the blank canvas Bishop Scanlan had left him, effecting nothing less than a transformation of the building into the spectacular edifice we see today.

Bishop Glass's partner in the renovation of both St. Vincent's and the Cathedral of the Madeleine was the great American architect John Theodore Comes. Born in Luxembourg, Comes immigrated to America as a boy and attended parochial school in St. Paul, Minnesota. It is believed that he studied architecture with Ralph Adams Cram, one of the country's foremost architects who had served as president of the American Institute of Architects. Comes practiced his profession as the senior partner in the firm Comes and Imbs in Pittsburgh, where he was an active Catholic layman. Cram called Comes "strikingly able" and considered him principally responsible for the restoration of the Gothic style to Catholic church architecture in this country. Cram called Comes's 1923 death a "tragedy" and commended the bishops of Cleveland, Duluth, Fall River and, interestingly, Salt Lake City for having embraced Comes's Gothic revival.[7]

Comes's education, as well as his faith, speak out in a lecture directed to seminarians on "Catholic Art and Architecture," which he described as "the symbolic expression in music, painting, sculpture and architecture of the truth contained in the Catholic religion ... outline, form, color, rhythm, tone and melody must all subserve" a supreme supernatural end, suggesting as they do the transcendent beauties and mysteries of the Catholic faith. "The church of stone must be a speaking manifestation of the living church and her mysteries. The pictures on the walls and on the altars are not simply adornment for the pleasure of the eyes but for the heart a book full of instruction, a sermon full of Truth ... Art becomes a transmitter and preserver of great ideas for all ages." Stressing that the church represents more than the pride of the priest or the architect and the prestige of the community, Comes described it foremost as God's dwelling "dedicated to the honor and glory of Him who holds our destinies in the hollow of His hand." He understood that "Unless the Lord build the house, they labor in vain that build it."[8] He had in common with his friend Bishop Glass the fact that he was first a believer and then a builder.

The two men were not new friends. They had met coincidentally on the golf course and discovered their common love of architecture. While pastor of St. Vincent's in Los Angeles, Glass had hired Comes to design a major renovation which had turned out to be a great success, so he knew he was dealing not only with a kindred spirit but also with an architect with a proven ability.

Transformation of the Cathedral included elements ranging from the most mundane to the most sublime. In the former category was a redesign of the steam heating system and installation of scaffolding from which interior decoration could be accomplished. Although the exterior of the building was still in good condition, Bishop Glass replaced the double flight of steps that led straight up from the east and west to the main entrance with the angled staircase from South Temple presently in use. At the entrance to the steps at the right beneath the light fixture a metal plaque was installed with Bishop Glass's coat of arms, and on the other side an American eagle with the legend *E Pluribus Unum*. At the center of the first landing was installed a large plaque honoring the memory of Bishop Scanlan.

Another exterior alteration was replacement of the crude tympanum over the main portal into the cathedral. For its completion, John Comes chose the sculptor Francis Aretz of Pittsburgh with whom he had previously worked and who was developing a lofty reputation in his field. Aretz was the sculptor of the façade at St. Agnes Church in Pittsburgh and of the figure of St. Agnes in Carrara marble standing in its high altar. Born of Dutch parents in Aix-la-Chapelle, Germany, Aretz had studied under Karl Kraus, a professor in the Aix Polytechnical Institute. His first representation in the United States occurred in an exhibit at the Pittsburgh Architectural Association in late 1916. His tympanum for the Cathedral of the Madeleine was considered a masterly work executed in concrete. As the *Intermountain Catholic* described Aretz working in his decrepit Pittsburgh studio: "rising in a sweeping half circle to the height of the structure, stands the sculptor's model, in brown clay, a composite showing the figure of Christ backed by an encircled cross and surrounded by the four fathers of the church and the twelve apostles." Within two months, the article concluded, the concrete cast will be made from the model and installed in Salt Lake City. At the same time will be created "smaller works for the two small doors in the façade and two life-size statues of Saints Peter and Paul." (Those two statues are above the side altars of St. Mary and St. Joseph, respectively, inside the Cathedral.) Aretz described his style as "absolute decoration without any naturalistic treatment." The great art of the future, he predicted, is to come from America; he deplored the modern tendency to copy the styles of previous ages.[9]

The two smaller panels Aretz mentions are, above the west side entrance, symbols of the seven sacraments, and above the east side entrance, the seven Gifts of the Holy Spirit. In the tympanum over the center portal Christ is represented as High Priest, clothed in priestly garments and flanked by two angels holding shields with emblems meaning "The Beginning and the End" on one side, and "Jesus the Saviour of Men" on the other. The twelve apostles, six standing and six kneeling, holding their appropriate symbols, occupy the field on either side of Our Lord. The four great Doctors of the Western Church, Saints Augustine, Gregory, Ambrose, and Jerome, complete this entourage in whose spiritual company the worshipper enters the Cathedral.

The only other major modification of the original Cathedral, visible from outside at the rear of the building, was removal of the five stained glass windows in the sanctuary. Those windows were among those executed by F. X. Zettler in Munich, from which it is believed they were shipped piecemeal to Salt Lake City for assembly in 1906. They depicted the Sorrowful Mysteries of the Rosary and were designed in unison with the windows on the west representing the Joyful Mysteries and those on the east representing the Glorious Mysteries. The nave windows measure 40' x 6' in size, while the transept windows measure 35' x 16'. The sanctuary windows were the same size as those in the nave. Unlike those on the west and east, though, the sanctuary windows did not follow the order of the rosary mysteries so that the Crucifixion could be placed in the center, above the altar. Accordingly, the mysteries appeared in the following order from left to right as one faced the altar: The Agony in the Garden, The Scourging at the Pillar, The Crucifixion, The Crowning with Thorns, and The Carrying of the Cross.[10]

As previously noted, Bishop Glass's taste in art rejected the realistic style of the Zettler windows in conformity with the contemporary doctrine that realism was inappropriate for purely decorative art, which should instead be symbolic.[11] Although he had hoped to replace them all, budgetary considerations limited him only to the sanctuary windows. The three central ones were removed and the spaces plastered over for murals, while the two outer windows were replaced with smaller ones featuring symbols of the twelve apostles executed by George Sotter of Pittsburgh. At this writing, the design and the disposition of the removed windows remain historical mysteries; no photographs have been found that show the scenes depicted in the windows in acceptable detail, and no documentation has been found of their sale or destruction.

To execute the murals that would replace the sanctuary windows, architect Comes recommended Felix Lieftuchter, an artist he had worked with in decorating St. Agnes Church in Cleveland, Ohio. It was there that Bishop Glass met him when he participated in the dedication ceremonies, and it became readily apparent to all three men that they shared a similar artistic vision. "Mr. Comes and I had the same ideas and feelings about art. He liked my work and we did several churches together," Lieftuchter recalled, adding that he considered Comes the "first good church architect in the United States."[12] In September 1916 Lieftuchter signed a contract to complete the murals by March 21, 1917, and though the job took a good deal longer, Bishop Glass and Comes were pleased enough with the results that they kept paying him ($9,216 all told) until November 20, 1917. "Lieftuchter says it's taking a great deal more time than he figured on," Comes reported to the bishop on April 18, "but I think he will stick and do a good job."[13]

Lieftuchter had been born in Cincinnati of German parents who returned to their native land for five years when the artist was fifteen years old. During that time he studied at the Royal Academy in Munich and travelled throughout Europe studying the great churches. "That's where I got my ideas," he recalled. "The paintings of saints in the Cathedral [of the Madeleine] are somewhat my general impression of what a church should be like. The architecture has a great deal to do with how you design art work."[14]

In his mid-thirties at the time, the young artist had signed the Cathedral contract before he even saw the building. As he had done no fresco work at the time, he elected to depart from tradition in the medieval European churches and paint in oil instead. In order to kill some of the acoustical resonance of the church, three to six layers of absorbent felt were first attached to the walls and canvas stretched over it, giving Lieftuchter the surface on which he needed to paint.[15] Then that surface was covered with oil-based Dutch Boy white lead paint—all materials having been purchased in Salt Lake City. For the figures themselves, "I first sketched the designs on paper and then enlarged them. All figures are about nine feet tall. To transfer the drawings to the wall, I drew them the proper size. We then perforated them around the main outlines and rubbed the paper with pulverized charcoal. This gave us the outline on the wall. I perforated the drawings with a tracing wheel such as one uses in sewing or else with a needle." Not surprisingly, the work was arduous. "I spent six to seven hours a day painting while I was doing the work over the altar. Sometimes I got very tired."[16]

In designing the figures, Lieftuchter became frustrated at the lack of professional models in Salt Lake City, but he solved his problem in an amusing manner. During the year he spent in the city, he befriended a family living on the Avenues behind the Cathedral. The mother was very beautiful and so were her two daughters who were attending the University of Utah. One evening at dinner, as Lieftuchter explained his problem obtaining models, the mother offered to allow one of her daughters to work in that capacity. Even when Lieftuchter pointed out that it would be

Fig. 15: Felix Lieftuchter, Cathedral mural artist, in later life.

necessary for the model to work in the nude, the parents still consented. Each day when the daughter would come to the artist's studio in the Cathedral basement, either the mother or daughter would be present as a chaperone. The faces of each of his figures, however, were painted out of the artist's imagination rather than from life.

The actual design of the panels was left almost entirely up to the artist. "The bishop suggested one or two of the figures for the paintings," he recalled, but "the actual design was always my own original idea. I never copy my paintings from anything. In the Cathedral of the Madeleine I selected nearly all the saints to be portrayed myself. Too often bishops and priests will choose subjects unsuited to the space." A photograph made of Lieftuchter and one of his portraits in Mexico City late in his life shows that he had the skill to create highly realistic and detailed likenesses, but he deliberately put aside realism for his work on the Cathedral. As the *Salt Lake Tribune* reported in an interview with him as the project neared completion, Lieftuchter shared Bishop Glass's idea that realism had no place in church art that was purely decorative: "No attempt has been made, Mr.

Lieftuchter explains, at any realistic effects. The work being decorative, the artist avoided realism in order to carry out the proper conventional forms of decorative art."[15]

Redecoration of the interior almost dictated that the Stations of the Cross (fourteen paintings or sculptures depicting episodes in the passion of Christ and situated around the walls of the church as objects of devotion, particularly during the season of Lent) be replaced. To execute that project, Bishop Glass contracted with artist Robert S. Chase of Boston, stipulating that his work must be approved by architect Comes and architectural expert Ralph Adams Cram. Most people would probably agree that Chase's work was the least successful of the redecoration efforts. The contract specified that the paintings "must be carefully studied and composed into color schemes to be harmonized in color and toned down to produce a quiet, dignified effect." In fact, they struck many observers as rather murky and gloomy, and even Cathedral historian Dwyer, while complimenting them on being "beautifully conceived," admits that they were "perhaps too dark for the Cathedral."[17] Still others, like Cathedral stalwart parishioner Decker Little, who removed the Scanlan stations to make way for the new ones, lamented that the old ones "had figures that stood out beautifully against the pure white Cathedral walls."

And that was not the end of the Stations' misfortunes. At a later time a traveling painter, eventually found to be of questionable credentials, was commissioned to repaint the halos on the Stations. Using potter's clay as a base, he applied an inexpensive gilt paint to the halos and to some of the scroll work and other embellishments throughout the church. Some years later, Salt Lake City artist Norman Smith restored the original appearance of the Stations by undoing that defective work. The project took some eighteen weeks. Working atop a ladder, Smith painstakingly etched off the gilt paint and the clay base and then matched the original color and technique. He had to be meticulously careful and claims that a close scrutiny of the Stations would reveal some of the defective painting.[18]

Bishop Glass fared much better with the sculptors he hired. One was Henry Schmitt of Buffalo, New York, one of America's foremost ecclesiastical sculptors, who with his son executed the three lindenwood statues of St. Anthony of Padua, St. Vincent de Paul, and Our Lady of Lourdes. Other sculptors whose names are not known also worked in the Cathedral.

Fig. 16: Our Lady of Lourdes shrine, west transept (later Our Lady of Guadalupe).

A father and son pair, believed not to be the Schmitts, left an ingenious signature to their work. It is said that when they completed their carvings there was no place to sign their names, so they each took a piece of wood and carved the other's likeness, then attached them to the sedilia in the sanctuary.

Isaac Kirchmayer, "one of the ablest American wood-carvers of the early twentieth century," carved the statues and reredos on the altars.[19] The linen folds on his carvings are a Kirchmayer trademark. On the transept altars the carving is done in oak, with various ornamental features highlighted in gold trim. Figures of adoring angels are painted on wood panels surrounding the panels. Architectural historian Ralph Adams Cram was so impressed with Kirchmayer's work that he and Comes both employed him at times, and Cram referred to Kirchmayer as "that amazing craftsman out of the fifteenth century, living and thinking and working in the twentieth century."[20]

A necessary part of any church designed in a medieval style is its bells. Bishop Glass contracted with the McShane Bell Company for two bells to be cast at the Maryland Brass Foundry, one weighing 2,650 pounds tuned to E-flat, and a smaller one of 1,300 pounds tuned to G. The bells were a gift to the Cathedral of Mrs. Joseph Geoghegan in memory of her husband. The larger was named Joseph and the smaller one Mary. A Latin inscription on the larger bell translates as "The thunderbolts I scatter; I ring in the Sabbath; I hustle the sluggards; I drive away storms; I proclaim peace after bloodshed," while the one on the smaller bell reads, ""I praise the true God; I call the people; I assemble the clergy; I bewail the dead; I disperse storm clouds; I do honor to feasts." Bishop Glass blessed the bells as "the voice calling the people to prayer, a voice also of either sorrow or joy."[21] Indeed the bells eloquently express, in only two musical notes, the entire gamut of emotions from sorrow to jubilance, serving like nothing else as the voice of the Utah Catholic community.

Inside the church, that voice is the organ. Bishop Scanlan had installed a Kimball organ in the choir loft in 1908 at a cost of approximately $25,000. In 1920 the organ was enhanced by the addition of a specially constructed harp stop and a set of chimes. The organ pipes had been carefully designed to frame the F. X. Zettler rose window donated by the Altar Society in 1906 and depicting St. Cecelia, Patroness of music, surrounded by twelve angels holding various instruments. Unfortunately, as Father Dwyer pointed out in his history of the Cathedral, the action on the organ reflected a transitional period between mechanical and electrical mechanisms, in which rubberized cloth was used for the stops. In time, the cloth would harden and crack, and the stops would not work, so the organ became inoperable for a period of years. In 1936 it was replaced by a Hammond electric organ, but in 1952 Father Dwyer had the original organ restored in memory of his parents.

Continuing the tradition of music established by Bishop Scanlan, Bishop Glass brought Professor Phillip Bambach from St. Vincent's in Los Angeles to become music director and organist upon the retirement of Nora Gleason in August 1916, after her twenty-six years of service to the Cathedral.

The first appearance of the boys sanctuary choir, seated in the choir stalls, took place in March 1917. The regular Cathedral choir attracted some members of long tenure. One, Walter Aures, began singing in the choir in the early 1920s and continued down to the mid-1960s. Born in 1889, he had been baptized in the original St. Mary's, perhaps by Bishop Scanlan himself. At the age of six or seven years, his sister had begun to sing in the Junior Choir of twelve to fifteen girls who sang a Low Mass on Sunday mornings. The adult choir traditionally sang the High Mass; both were under the direction of Nora Gleason who, with the Sisters of the Holy Cross, trained the well-known Cathedral organist Ethel Hogan Hanson Heinz Merrill, thus passing along the Cathedral's music tradition at the organ console as well as in the choir.

The renovation project moved on toward completion. Reminiscent of the Middle Ages, gargoyles were installed on the steeples. On the Gothic cathedrals of medieval times, these figures served as disguises to waterspouts. Over the years they evolved into complex and grotesque structures carved by stonecutters and sculptors for installation in the buttresses as downspouts. When it rained, the frightening creatures would appear to be spitting water onto the ground below. The figures were not only decorative, but, in times of widespread illiteracy, also didactic, reminding the sinner of the waiting Inferno and credibly depicting the horrors of damnation. Bishop Glass's gargoyles, however, were strictly ornamental. Over the following years, they deteriorated and eroded to the degree that they either weathered away or, having become hazardous, were removed in 1930; after which they were apparently lost. As shall be seen, new gargoyles were installed in the exterior renovation of 1977.

Both architect and rector must have been relieved to see the restoration finally accomplished. It had proved a daring and demanding project, taxing the talents of both. An early figure on the overall cost of the redecoration totaled $104,287, though the actual amount was eventually determined to be $130,000. Thus, Bishop Glass and architect Comes left the imprint of their time on the interior of the Cathedral just as Bishop Scanlan and architects Neuhausen and Mecklenburg had left their imprint on the exterior.

The responsibility had been tremendous for Bishop Glass and one that was not always comprehended by those among his flock who still felt the contrast between this handsomely attired prelate who maintained his residence in Federal Heights (the only Salt Lake City bishop prior to Bishop Weigand to have his own home apart from the Cathedral rectory), and his sometimes shabbily dressed predecessor, who had been known to go without the necessities of life. Bishop Glass's detractors would call his artistic judgment untrained and criticize the financial management and fiscal record of his administration. To that his devotees would reply that it was with funds from his own father's estate that he purchased his home, and that he was generous to his fellow priests and friends with the $750 monthly allotment given him by the Doheny family as a gift upon the twenty-fifth anniversary of his ordination to the priesthood. They admired his perseverance, despite the difficulty he must have found in adjusting to the more primitive way of life in Salt Lake City after the comforts of St. Vincent's in Los Angeles. At any rate, it is agreed by all that Bishop Glass sincerely dedicated the remainder of his life to a diocese that was generally not considered one of the best of environments for Catholicism.

Memories of green pillars and white plaster walls within the Cathedral yielded reluctantly to the vibrant colors of the redecoration. Originally concerned with mere survival in the Scanlan days, Utah Catholics now came to feel what Comes called the "quasi-divine hand of art." The new darker purple tones expressed Comes's belief that such hues encouraged an atmosphere of prayer more than a brighter interior would. But the colors also enhanced a higher degree of liturgical pageantry than the simpler décor of the Scanlan interior, and a new liturgical tradition began to emerge. Among the celebrations was the annual Forty-Hour Devotion processions in which the young school children, holding baskets of rose petals on one arm, gently dropped them one by one as they came up the center aisle. And, a new system of pew rentals encouraged a greater sense of engagement of the parishioners with the church. Some of the original family names could still be seen at the pew entrances long after the rental system had been abandoned, and a few parishioners would continue to occupy the same pews they chose many years ago.

The concept of the Cathedral as an Old World shrine revives the vision of an apotheosis, as meaningful today as it was when Lieftuchter painted it into his murals. Myth is basic to his theme as well as to the symbolism within the Cathedral. In the Cathedral myths flourish as secret sources of spiritual energy. There is simplicity in some: the chalice, shocks of grain and grapes for the Eucharist; the dove for the Holy Spirit. The pelican, tearing open her breast to feed her young with her own life blood, alludes to the atonement of Christ upon the cross. The eagle with young seen in the medallion of the Ascension window symbolizes the gospel taking flight to all the world. The peacock in the Assumption window tells of eternal life, resurrection and immortality in the annual renewal of its beautiful plumage. An extended allegory of the Annunciation is found in the unicorn, a small animal surprisingly fierce and swift, with a sharp, single horn in the center of its forehead. Supposedly no hunter could capture it by force, but it could be taken by trickery. The hunter had to lead a virgin to a spot frequented by the unicorn and leave her alone there. According to the myth, the unicorn would sense her purity and run to her, lay its head in her lap and fall asleep. Thus its capture would be effected. The unicorn became symbolic of purity in general and feminine chastity in particular.

The imagery of the Four Evangelists (gleaned from Ezekiel 1:5–10, 10:19–22, and Revelation 4:7 and featured in gold at the base of the four spandrels reaching to the heights of the sanctuary) shows Mark as a winged lion to emphasize the Resurrection. The newborn lion cub appears to be dead, but after three days it is licked into wakefulness by its father. Luke is the winged ox, signifying sacrificial death; John is the eagle soaring to the throne of grace; and Matthew is seen as a winged man because his Gospel dwells more on the human side of Christ than do the other Gospels.

Fig. 17: Bishop Glass in Rome, 1925.

Day and night, Scripture says, these Evangelists continually praise God. The sanctuary itself becomes the scene of the mystical sacrifice of Calvary wherein the Mass will gather all creation from east to west in adoration. The words, "Christ Died for All" are inscribed in the center panel above the high altar.

The Agnus Dei medallion in the Nativity window in the west nave is more than a simple symbol; it is a sacramental, an object which is the means of receiving actual grace to do good, avoid evil, and protect body and soul. It implies the unity in man of matter and spirit and, in this case, is a small flat piece of wax impressed with the figure of a lamb on which is superimposed a cross or banner. The wax is white and pure like the virgin flesh of Christ, and the lamb a sign of a victim offered in sacrifice. Sin and death are victims of our Lord. The "great consecrations" of Agnus Dei take place only in the first year of each Pontiff's reign and every seventh year thereafter. On the Wednesday of Easter Week, pieces of wax prepared by monks are brought to the Pope, who dips them in water and chrism and balsam with appropriate prayers. They are distributed the following Saturday when the Pope, after the Agnus Dei of the Mass, places a packet of them into the inverted mitre of each cardinal and bishop present. Remaining ones are sent to prelates and religious communities in all parts of the world. The efficacy of this sacramental derives from its representation of our Lord as sacrificial victim.

Bishop Glass's renovation of the Cathedral is all the more remarkable considering the energy he had left over for a vigorous involvement in other diocesan developments as well as other civic and ecclesiastical responsibilities. To understand his work on the Cathedral, one should be aware of those simultaneous involvements.

One of those was a dramatic expansion of the diocese in the number of priests, parishes and missions. During his tenure, the number of parishes doubled from ten to twenty, while the number of priests roughly tripled: in 1919 there had been only eight priests incardinated (assigned to the diocese), with twelve borrowed from other dioceses. By the time of the bishop's death in 1926, there were twenty-three incardinated and only five borrowed.

Many diocesan organizations trace their origin to the Cathedral parish during Bishop Glass's time. The Catholic Woman's League started in 1916. The Bishop successfully requested the Pope to recognize Mrs. A. H. S. Bird with a medal decoration instituted by Pope Leo XIII in 1888 as *Pro Ecclesia et Pontifice* for her service as President of the Catholic Woman's League of Salt Lake City and Vice President of the National Council of Catholic Women. She was the first American woman to receive that honor.[22] Other organizations dating from the Glass era include the St. Vincent de Paul Society (1920), the Escalante Club and the Catholic Men's Club (both 1924), the Catholic Business Women's Club (1917), later the Meynell Club (1922), and the Newman Club (1920).

Catholic education also felt Bishop Glass's touch. Although, despite his best efforts, he was forced to close All Hallows College in 1918, he opened Judge Memorial in 1920 and a Cathedral School in the basement in 1921. Although St. Mary of the Wasatch did not open until after his

Fig. 18: A reliquary brought to the Cathedral from Europe by Bishop Glass.

death in 1926, he selected and blessed the site of the school.

In some ways a man before his times liturgically, Bishop Glass was known to be partial to congregational singing. He invited Professor Amedee Tremblay, a noted Canadian composer and organist at the Catholic Basilica in Ottawa, to assist in the musical direction at the Cathedral. Upon the retirement of Nora Gleason, Bishop Scanlan's long-time organist whom he had plucked from the mining camps of southern Utah and provided her musical education in Salt Lake City and Chicago, Bishop Glass made the audacious move of replacing her with her fourteen-year-old student Ethel Hogan, surely the youngest principal organist in the history of the Cathedral. Hogan became as much of an institution at the Cathedral as Gleason had been, serving as organist until 1973.

Bishop Glass's last contributions to the Cathedral and the diocese came during his trip to Rome in 1924–25. In August 1924 he wrote a general letter to the clergy and people of the diocese, pointing out that never, during the thirty-seven years since Utah had been made an Apostolic Vicariate in 1887, had a bishop made an *ad limina* visit to Rome to report to the Pope on diocesan affairs. He announced that he had booked passage on a ship departing from New York on September 27.[23] Although he made no mention of it at the time, in the light of subsequent events there is a possibility that his faltering health was a factor in his decision, both because he may have realized this would be his last chance to visit Rome, or because he may have hoped that the salubrious climate and restful visits to places he had enjoyed on other occasions might prove restorative. The visit became a prolonged vacation lasting approximately a year.

The *ad limina* visit to Rome was only a part of his itinerary, which included visits to various churches and other sites in France. His travels included a quest for a relic of St. Mary Magdalene, which he acquired at the Church of St. Maximin in southern France where her remains were kept. In Florence he acquired the Cigoli painting of St. Mary Magdalene, supposedly dating to the early seventeenth century, and which is now installed above the Cathedral altar. Other acquisitions included a collection of statuary, carvings, and some forty paintings which he thought to be both originals and copies of works by Renaissance artists. From Switzerland, the bishop brought back a set of rich pontifical vestments made partially with thread of gold. Their splendor enriched the beauty of religious services in the Cathedral and cemented Bishop Glass's image as a true Prince of the Church.

Although Bishop Glass returned from Europe in better health than he had left, he soon took a turn for the worse and left for Los Angeles in a continuing but futile effort to recover. It was there that he was diagnosed with cancer and died on January 26, 1926. His funeral obsequies, which lasted from January 30 to February 2 at the Cathedral, were attended by civic and ecclesiastical dignitaries from Utah and the nation. A bishop's remains are ordinarily interred in the last diocese over which he had presided, but Bishop Glass, as a member of the Congregation of the Mission, was buried in his order's cemetery in Los Angeles.

At Mount Calvary Cemetery in Salt Lake City, a stone marker was erected with a bronze crucifix, on an incline atop the circular plot with the altar upon which the incumbent bishop celebrates Mass each Memorial Day. The handsome memorial overlooks first the burial places of Bishop Glass's fellow priests and religious; then, beyond, slanting downward, those of the souls he served; and finally the beautiful city rolling out across the valley. It is close enough to the Cathedral to hear the bells sounding on the quarter hour. The renovated Cathedral, representing the "combined expression of the enduring strength of Bishop Scanlan and the artistic talent and aesthetic spirit of Bishop Glass," is his lasting monument, transformed now from the Cathedral of St. Mary Magdalene to the Cathedral of the Madeleine as life itself can be transformed under the redeeming touch of the Master.[24]

Fig. 19: Bishops Mitty and Hunt, perhaps at the time of Bishop Hunt's episcopal ordination.

Chapter 3

Redemption

"There was a man named John sent by God." (John 1:6)

Bishop Scanlan was an Irishman, but he had been elevated to the episcopacy from within the Utah clergy. It would be a long time before that happened again—in 1937, when Bishop Duane G. Hunt was ordained—and to the date of this writing we have not yet had another "native" bishop.[1] Bishop Glass, of course, was from Los Angeles, but the next two, both of whom served brief but important tenures bridging the gap between Glass and Hunt, were New Yorkers.

It would not, perhaps, be an exaggeration to say that Bishop John J. Mitty was a son of the church not only through his ordination, but even through his parentage, for his mother died when he was ten and his father when he was fourteen, leaving the Catholic school and the seminary he attended responsible for a large part of his upbringing. Born to Irish parents in Greenwich Village in 1884, he remembered his mother taking him at the age of eight or nine to the great seminary of Dunwoodie, which was then in the initial stage of construction (in fact only the foundation was visible). A watchman at the site explained what each part of the new building would be, whereupon Mrs. Mitty, perhaps aware of her impending demise, told her son, "I hope that some day you will come here."

He did. After attending a Christian Brothers school and graduating from Manhattan College, he entered Dunwoodie and was ordained in

1906 by John Cardinal Farley of New York. Graduate studies followed, with work at Catholic University in Washington, D.C., the Pontifical Seminary in Rome from which he received his Doctorate of Divinity, and further work at the University of Munich. Dunwoodie reentered his life at that point, and he served as Professor of Dogmatic Theology there for eight years.

World War I was a defining experience for him, as The Great War was for the entire generation. When the United States entered the war in 1917, he enlisted in the 49th Regiment at Camp Merritt, New Jersey and became chaplain of the 101st Infantry, a unit of the famed 26th "Yankee Division." He saw action in the Meuse-Argonne offensive and was discharged with the rank of First Lieutenant. The rigors of military life seemed to fit well with the tough existence he no doubt had experienced as an orphan; for the rest of his life as a priest he was so well known for his own discipline and the regimentation he expected of his subordinates that he was given the nickname "Iron John."

His postwar life saw a change from academia to parish ministry. His first pastorate was Sacred Heart parish in Highland Hills, New York which included the chaplaincy at the United States Military Academy at West Point, situated within the parish boundaries. It was there that he reportedly became acquainted with Gen. Douglas MacArthur, the hero of the Pacific Theater of World War II, who was then Superintendent of the Academy. Three years later he was appointed pastor of St. Luke's parish in the Bronx, and it was while there, on June 21, 1926 that he received his papal appointment to the Diocese of Salt Lake.

At the age of thirty-two, Mitty was one of the youngest men ever elevated to the American hierarchy. Following his ordination by Patrick Cardinal Hayes at St. Patrick's Cathedral, a dinner was held in his honor at the Hotel Commodore. In his afterdinner comments, the young bishop showed his youthful enthusiasm for the task ahead. "His Eminence [Cardinal Hayes] may have the greatest diocese," he said, "but I have the largest. I serve notice here and now to all present that Salt Lake's aim is not merely to be the largest but also the greatest Diocese in the country." Cardinal Hayes evidently had a better idea of the magnitude of the problems Mitty would face in Salt Lake City, for in his reply he reported that the young bishop had always wanted to be a missionary in some far-off land, and "now his dream has come true." Rather than making the Diocese of Salt Lake the greatest in the country, a much more proximate problem was simply getting it solvent, and as things turned out, he did not completely reach even that much more modest goal.

A month later at his impressive installation at the Cathedral of the Madeleine, he undertook what he called the change from "the Borough of the Bronx to the ways of the West." Calling upon the help of St. Mary Magdalene "to whom this Diocese and this people are dedicated," he prayed that "the spirit of Bishop Scanlan and Bishop Glass [may] watch over and protect us." Over the next six years, he would no doubt find many occasions to invoke the spirit of frugality embodied by Bishop Scanlan, while he might have prayed for a little less intense visitation from the spendthrift spirit of his immediate predecessor.

Nothing, in fact, was more insistent than the indebtedness left behind by Bishop Glass. As we have seen, although Bishop Glass may have been a poor financial administrator, he was generous with his personal resources, gladly sharing them with his priests and using them to pay bills, so that he never asked his fellow Utah Catholics to undertake a financial burden that he himself was not willing to shoulder. Fortunately for the diocese, his successor was every bit as generous with his own money. A mere two months after his consecration in Salt Lake City, the young bishop wrote to his friend Patrick Cardinal Hayes with a dire report on the financial condition of the diocese: "Unfortunately Bishop Glass never took anyone into his confidence and no one knows anything about the finances; he had the habit of taking out notes and in many cases I cannot find out for what purpose.... In addition to notes the poor Bishop had a mania for buying houses and real estate which are not usable and for which we could not get the money he paid."

Bishop Mitty found it necessary to expend whatever ordination gifts and other monies he had to stave off the most insistent creditors: "I have been thanking God for the purse from the New York clergy and other donations I received in New York as they have enabled me to meet pressing obligations and keep out of jail [!]. As far as I can see the future for my own personal finances, I shall have to depend for room and board upon the

Cathedral and live on intentions because every cent I can lay my hands on from all sources will have to go to satisfy diocesan obligations."[2]

Obviously, though, such funds were one-time resources and could serve only as a stopgap until regular donations from Utah Catholic laypeople could be generated. In order to do that, the bishop summoned the men of the diocese to a meeting at the Cathedral on May 14, 1928.[3] His notes for his speech that evening, which are extant in the Diocesan Archives, are one of the most remarkable documents in Utah Catholic history, for they constitute a relentless tongue-lashing supported by irrefutable financial data, and vividly illustrate how Bishop Mitty acquired his "Iron John" nickname.

"These remarks are confidential and not to be published," he began. "I am going to talk very frankly, straight from the shoulder, but I intend to say my say. I shall give you an opportunity at the end to ask questions." Thereupon followed an amazing litany of financial apathy and incompetence throughout the diocese: "Parishes with debts for years. Never any principal paid. Some parishes for years borrowing money to pay interest on debt." Priests' salaries were a disgrace, averaging $441 per year. "The homes of some priests are a disgrace. Laity have decent places; any hole good enough for a priest. Sickness of priests due to a lack of proper nourishment and to lack of vacations, and due to overwork. Wonder they don't leave."

Annual incomes of Utah parishes, he calculated, point to an average donation of $8.50 per person; contributions to diocesan expenses were even worse, averaging from 6 ½ cents per person to fifteen cents over a three-year period. "You can judge, then," he concluded, "that the diocese does not receive enough income to pay the ordinary running expenses of the diocese," adding that all of the money received at the time of his ordination has been given to the diocese. "I have received absolutely no salary nor compensation of any kind since I have come. Any donations given me have been turned over to the diocese."

Although Bishop Mitty, as we have seen, was well aware of Bishop Glass's shortcomings as a fiscal administrator, he was not about to give that to his audience as an excuse for their own shortcomings. After pointing out that Cathedral finances, for example, were administered by a lay committee outside Bishop Glass's control, and that the debt incurred by them was not his fault, Mitty added, "I trust that this statement will kill once for all any of the back stairs whispering about Bishop Glass' squandering diocesan money. You did not give him any to squander, you did not give him enough for routine expenses. Any money he did spend was given to him by personal friends and not by you."

Nor were the problems the bishop observed in the diocese confined to financial matters, for the respect rendered by Catholic laypeople to the bishop and clergy were equally deplorable. "No matter what my own personal inclinations are in these matters, there is a certain respect due to my position as Bishop. It is part of my job to train you if you show a lack of it." Mitty reserved a particular vitriol of the Catholic people of Salt Lake City: "Whatever your opinion of yourselves may be the opinion of the clergy in which I concur is that, with the exception of one or two organizations, you are the most difficult and most unresponsive group of Catholic people any of us has ever had to deal with. I have had a varied experience and I never came in contact with a more difficult group ... . You are subnormal and way below par." "We have come to the crossing of the roads," Bishop Mitty concluded. "Things cannot go on in this way."

Over subsequent years, the May 14 meeting became a legendary episode in Utah Catholic history as those in attendance shared their memories and passed them down to later generations. The overwhelming recollection was of Bishop Mitty as a stern drill sergeant dressing down his miscreant troops. It would be difficult to imagine, in the face of all that harsh rhetoric, that many in the audience were happy to have heard what they did, but subsequent developments prove that they did get the message. No doubt moved by the bishop's own monetary sacrifice and his reformation of diocesan financial practices, the Catholic laity decided they could once again trust that their donations would be wisely administered, and collections went up dramatically: the fund for radio broadcasting, which had been a mere $10 annually in 1926 and 1927, swelled to $968.72 in 1928, while the Seminary Collection, which had averaged an annual $742 since 1916, became $3,611.78 in 1929. That increase in funding enabled Utah's first native-born priest, Fr. Robert J. Dwyer, to be ordained in 1932 during the interregnum between Bishops Mitty and Kearney.[4] Perhaps inspired by their bishop's example of hard work and discipline, there were no fewer than nineteen Utah seminarians preparing for ordination, as

Fig. 20: Bishop James E. Kearney.

we have noted, by the time Mitty left Utah.[5] "In short order," Bernice Maher Mooney observes, "he had turned the diocese into one of the best organized in the United States. He left an authentic priestly imprint upon the Cathedral of the Madeleine and took from it what he had absorbed therein of 'the saintly heroic Bishop Scanlan and the gentle, cultured

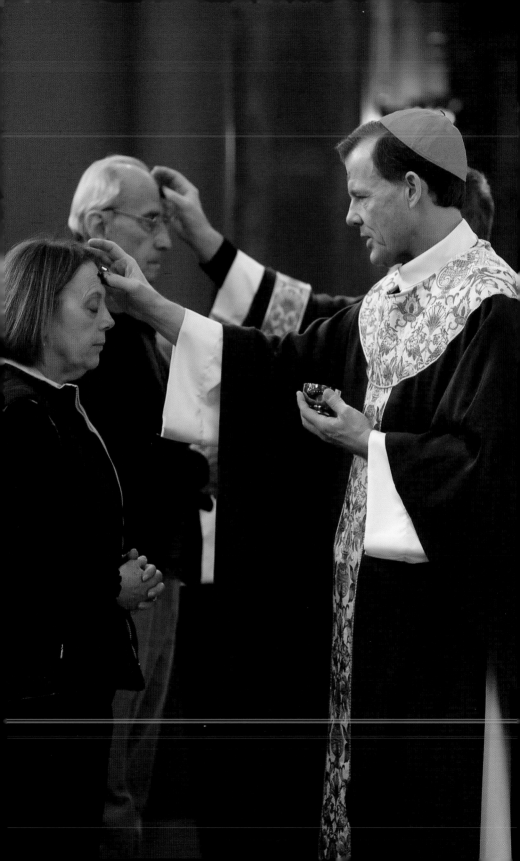

Bishop Glass to whom it has been my daily prayer that I might be a worthy successor'."[6]

As much progress as Bishop Mitty accomplished, though, he was destined to leave the projects of fiscal solvency and ecclesiastical maturity unfinished. There is some evidence that Bishop Mitty had been given to understand that his episcopacy in Salt Lake City would be a relatively brief one in which he would move the diocese out of its emergency status and then be called to other things. What those "other things" might be became apparent in April 1932 when Monsignor Duane G. Hunt was directed to read in the Cathedral the papal bull relieving Bishop Mitty of the jurisdiction of Salt Lake City and appointing him Coadjutor Bishop of San Francisco to assist the aging Archbishop Hanna. Hanna himself was present on the occasion, as were Utah Governor George Dern, representatives from Fort Douglas, and the clergy and laity who had come to respect and admire, if not always, perhaps, to love, their disciplined and outspoken bishop. The chant *Ecce Sacerdos* filled the Cathedral, then Monsignor Hunt reminded the attendees that "The appraisal of Bishop Mitty's work is no eulogy, but a mere recital of the facts of the accomplishments of his administration in Salt Lake City, a record of prudence, economy and progress."[7]

Although Mitty's successor, James E. Kearney, was also a New Yorker, the two bishops could hardly have been more different in almost every way. Where Mitty had imposed a near military regime on the diocese, Kearney was a jovial Irishman who was known to punctuate his homilies with Irish folk songs. Where Mitty had been a rather aloof figure who elicited respect perhaps more than love, Kearney loved human contact and enjoyed teaching his people with slide shows that he had designed. Both bishops, though, were disciplined financial managers and fund raisers, and it was Bishop Kearney's great achievement to finish paying off the Cathedral debt that Bishop Mitty had inherited.

Although James E. Kearney had been born in Red Oak, Iowa, to William and Rosina O'Doherty Kearney in 1884, the family moved to New York when the boy was only two years old, and he considered himself a native New Yorker. He attended Clinton High School and graduated from Teachers College in New York. Like Bishop Mitty, he attended St. Joseph Seminary in Dunwoodie before being ordained in 1908. He served as pastor of the Church of the Holy Rosary in Manhattan for several years, then returned to school at Catholic University of America, where he received the licentiate in Sacred Theology. Once again like Bishop Mitty, he spent some time in academia, serving as professor of religion at Good Counsel College in White Plains, New York, and also teaching at Cathedral College. Then it was back to parish ministry, where he served as assistant pastor and school director of St. Cecelia's Church in Manhattan. Lastly, he established St. Francis Xavier Parish in the Bronx and supervised the Catholic schools of that borough. He was ordained Bishop of Salt Lake on July 4, 1932, his forty-eighth birthday.

His first day in his new diocese portended humor and happiness, which came to characterize his brief episcopacy. When he got off the train, he was met by an enthusiastic throng of local Catholics and the band from Notre Dame School in Price, which welcomed him by playing "The Sidewalks of New York." The poetry-loving bishop responded with a bit of humorous verse:

> Thank God for the bitter and ceaseless strife,
> For the sting of the chastening rod …
> Thank God for the joys, for the grief of life,
> And oh! Thank God for God.

Unfortunately, the welcome at the station was eating into his schedule for the day, and he had to rush off to avoid being late for his first Mass at the Cathedral. As it was, he vested hurriedly in the rectory, and caught his first view of his new cathedral as he walked in procession down the center aisle, tears streaming down his face as he was overcome with the beauty of the great structure.

Love of Utah Catholics for their bishop was warm and immediate, and the bishop warmly reciprocated. He loved to recite poetry to make a point in his homilies, and his illustrated lectures on subjects both religious and secular were popular. He lectured in the Cathedral on "The Life of Christ," at Weber College on "A Tour Through Europe," during Lent he depicted "The Passion of Christ," and at Christmas, "The Other Wise Man." In March 1935 he lectured the PTA at Judge Memorial on the

Fig. 21: Bishop Kearney accepts the check from Dr. John J. Galligan to retire the debt on the Cathedral, November 28, 1936.

Irish poet and songwriter Thomas Moore, on which occasion the diocesan newspaper reported that he "illustrated his lecture with several of Moore's most charming songs," accompanied by Cathedral organist Ethel Hogan Heinz Hanson on the piano.[8]

Bishop Kearney set out to complete the work of his predecessor to pay off the remaining $50,000 debt on the Cathedral. Like Bishop Mitty, he found that old friends and other Catholics in New York could be tapped for donations to help the beleaguered Utah diocese. He returned to his native state and spoke in churches, soliciting funds for Salt Lake City. As he launched his campaign at the beginning of 1935, he announced that "unless we select this time, in spite of depression, the problem in all likelihood will continue indefinitely." In addition to pledge cards distributed in the churches for requested donations of at least twenty-five dollars from each wage earner, Bishop Kearney pleaded with people to donate items of gold or silver which could be spared, with the goal of raising $3,750 a month to retire the debt by the end of the year.[9]

But canceling the debt was a slow and difficult process. By mid-November, seventy percent of the goal had been reached. A fair was held at Judge Memorial in early December, which brought the total to $38,810, an amount that, considering the Depression, was "generous in the extreme."[10] In April 1936 the people were called to a final spurt of action leading up to the last collection on November 15, at which time the bishop announced that the Cathedral would be consecrated debt-free on November 28, with Mass to be sung by Archbishop Mitty. Any remaining debt after November 15 would be assumed as the personal responsibility of Bishop Kearney.[11] His persistence and determination were reminiscent of the spirit in which Father Kelly first purchased ground to establish the Church of St. Mary Magdalene seventy years before.

The ceremony of consecration for the Cathedral, which was presided over by Amleto Giovanni Cicognani, Apostolic Delegate to the United States, was splendid in its symbolism. Holy chrism, oil of catechumens, water, salt, ashes, wine, and incense were employed to signify purity of heart, wisdom, penance, joy, and prayer. Twelve crosses were affixed to the inner walls of the church and fitted with twelve slender tapers. The crosses were anointed with the words, "May this temple be sanctified

Fig. 22: Crowd outside the Cathedral at the time of the rededication Mass.

and consecrated," and subsequently would be lighted only on the solemn festival of the anniversary of the day of consecration.

The ceremony opened with Bishop Kearney, in three successive processions around the church, sprinkling holy water, and pausing at the main entrance each time he passed it to knock at the door and say, "Lift up your gates ... and the King of Glory shall come in." Within, to the chanting of the Litany of the Saints by the priests' choir, the Bishop drew two transverse lines, in the form of a Greek cross, from the four corners of the church, using ashes, and marking in one a Greek letter signifying the Jews, and in another a Latin letter signifying the Gentiles.

In August, news of Bishop Kearney's elevation to the Episcopal See of Rochester, New York, succeeding Archbishop Mooney, send shocks of sorrow among his people. He set about farewell visitations, personally greeting every member of each congregation. The *Intermountain Catholic* asserted that he had "carved a niche for himself that will forever be a shrine."[12] The consecration of his successor, Bishop Duane G. Hunt, took place on the fifth anniversary of Bishop Kearney's own ascension to the Cathedral throne.

Fig. 23: Bishop Kearney enters the Cathedral for the rededication Mass.

The Cathedral of the Madeleine now stood as financially stable as its great stone edifice was physically solid. The ancient architecture continued to carry the good news of the Gospel into contemporary culture. But the Church is, at bottom, much more than its physical manifestation, for its life is grounded in the vibrant quality of its spirituality. The very need to fortify and strengthen faith itself seemed to call forth the commitment of the man who would come to be known as the Second Builder of the Diocese of Salt Lake City. The life of Duane Garrison Hunt, fifth Bishop of Salt Lake, in the words of Bishop Dwyer, provides an "enlightened commentary on the impact of Catholicism on the American mind."[13]

Born in 1884 in Reynolds, Nebraska, he was reared a Methodist by parents to whom he always remained grateful for their example of what he called "plain living and honest thinking. Devout Methodists, their faith was untinged with fanaticism, and they stood foursquare for all those principles of fundamental Christianity upon which the nation itself had been built." Through the Sunday School classes of his youth, he learned the basic doctrines of Christianity and the stories of the Bible. "In a word, during my adolescent years I was an avowed and professing Protestant, a thorough conformist." Though he had acquaintance with only one Catholic family who were, incidentally, exemplary people, "I swallowed in its entirety the general verdict of my friends and associates, that Catholics were a people on a lower social level than ourselves, ignorant and inferior, held in durance vile by the evil machinations of the hierarchy."[14]

While attending the Methodist Cornell College in Iowa, and his interest in Catholicism yet a ways in the future, he became frustrated with certain aspects of his Protestant culture, including extemporaneous prayers, testimony meetings, and what he regarded as an excessive negativism in prohibition of liquor, tobacco, card playing, and dancing. During a hiatus in his college work necessitated by a shortage of funds, he taught school in an Iowa community that had a Catholic Church, and began an idle program of reading Catholic literature. Finding it increasingly persuasive, he could not as yet, however, overcome his residual anti-Catholic prejudice, nor yet continue to accept the validity of his native Protestantism. The quandary continued through graduation and a teaching career in Iowa public schools. Eventually, while a student in the University of Iowa Law School, he came to a conversion based largely on intellectual grounds, largely influenced by Cardinal Newman's *Apologia Pro Vita Sua*. The liturgy and ceremonial of the Church played only a minor role in his conversion.

By 1912 he was informed that his eyes, which remained problematic throughout his adult life, would not stand the strain of the great amount of reading involved in the study of law. He changed his field to public speaking and enrolled at the University of Chicago. By then he was determined to enter the Catholic Church. He sought out the closest priest to his lodging, Father H. M. Shea, Assistant at the Church of St. Thomas the Apostle, with whom he studied catechism twice weekly. From then on, completing his conversion was easy: "My time for reading was limited, but the fundamentals were already so fixed in my mind that all the rest followed with the ease of completing a picture puzzle once the key had been discovered. I am afraid I was a disappointing convert to my instructor. My battles were all over before I had rung his door bell."[15] Although some of his Protestant friends argued with his decision all one night, the future bishop was baptized and received his first Holy Communion at age twenty-nine.

But more was soon to come, and rarely does one experience two life-changing events in such close succession. Hunt's baptism took place in January 1913, and that very spring the new convert accepted a teaching position at the University of Utah in Salt Lake City, the city in which he would spend the rest of his life and exert the most profound influence on its Catholic community. He was unable to appreciate the fatefulness of the move at the time, for he considered the job only a stepping stone to something better elsewhere: "The only plan I had … was to teach here a year or two and then take more post-graduate work in my newly chosen department, that of Public Speaking, looking to some higher scholastic degrees."[16]

But it was not to be. Very soon he discovered that his professorship was only a job, and that "the only thing that I was really interested in was the Catholic religion," how he could promote it and defend it and perhaps convince others to convert. In time he began understand those impulses as a call to the priesthood. Bishop Glass agreed to accept him as a seminarian. Duane G. Hunt attended St. Patrick's Seminary in Menlo Park, California, and was ordained by Bishop Glass for the Diocese of Salt Lake City in June 1920.[17] It was the first ordination to take place in the Cathedral of the Madeleine.

Significantly, the ordination took place a year before actual completion of his seminary program because of the urgent need for priests in the diocese. In fact, the new priest learned that there was no dearth of work for him, on the one hand, and that ecclesiastical advancement was readily available on the other. After a couple of years as Assistant at the Cathedral, he was sent for eight months to minister at the St. John of God mission in Vernal. Back in Salt Lake City, he was named Vice Rector in 1923, Rector in 1925, and at the same time elevated to the rank of Papal Chamberlain with the title Very Reverend Monsignor. In 1926 he became Chancellor of the Diocese and in 1928 Vicar General. Named Domestic Prelate with the title of Right Reverend Monsignor in 1929, he acted as administrator of the diocese during the interim between the transfer of Bishop Mitty and the appointment of Bishop Kearney. Finally, with the departure of Bishop Kearney, Msgr. Hunt was named the next bishop. Archbishop Mitty returned to Salt Lake City in 1937 to ordain his beloved assistant. It was a dizzying ascent up the ecclesiastical ladder.

The demeanor of the new bishop was deceiving. Outwardly, he appeared stern and austere, but inwardly he was especially caring and warm. Although rather short in physical height, he was, as Archbishop Dwyer observed in a tribute at the time of his death, a man of "unusual moral and intellectual stature."[18]

Four long years toward the beginning of Bishop Hunt's term as bishop were taken up by the greatest tragedy in world history to that point: World War II. From its outset, Bishop Hunt had appreciated the momentous nature of the struggle and took care to impress that upon Cathedral parishioners. In a letter he wrote to be read at all Masses the first Easter of the war, he said, "The wonderful edifice of Christian civilization, built by the Catholic Church through centuries of devotion and sacrifice, is now threatened with collapse. It is being dragged up the slopes of a new Calvary and prepared for crucifixion."[19] During the two years before the United States became militarily involved in the war, Bishop Hunt made sure the people of the Cathedral were involved in humanitarian efforts through fund drives for displaced people in Europe and for worldwide missions which had been dependent upon European Catholics for their support. Special days of prayer were designated, and Utah Catholics were admonished to invite into their homes Catholic young men from military bases in Utah.[20]

Similarly, once the United States found itself at war, Bishop Hunt was unflinching in his assessment of what the war was going to cost: "Let there be no illusions about the seriousness of the undertaking. Without doubt, we shall suffer; we shall suffer cruel losses, not only in property but, what is infinitely worse, in life. Many of our boys will not come home; they will be called upon to make the supreme sacrifice. Such suffering we must offer up to God as a penance. We must lay our gifts on the altar of patriotism." As men from the Cathedral enlisted in the various military branches, an "Honor Roll" of their names, which eventually reached 105, was posted in the vestibule of the church. Later, the bishop announced that "During the duration of the war, all the Catholics of this parish will receive Holy Communion on the First Sunday of each month. This Holy Communion will be offered as a special petition to Almighty God for the boys in the forces of the United States."[21]

One of the positive results of World War II was in the area of civil rights. Although troops of color fought in segregated units during the war, realization of their valiant service led President Harry Truman to order integration of the services afterward, and since that time the military has led the rest of the country in equal treatment of the races. Bishop Hunt was in the forefront of that movement. On February 14, 1943 he admonished that "The national problem has arisen concerning the Negro in this Community. These men wearing the uniform of the Army or Navy are fighting for the defense of democracy. Their uniform alone should solicit our respect, courtesy and any kindness we may be able to show them."[22]

As one would expect, Bishop Hunt constantly called upon the people of the Cathedral for special days of prayer and intercessions for servicemen and for the success of the Allied efforts. As the country prepared for the D-day invasion of France on June 6, 1944, the greatest concerted assault in world history, the bishop ordered all Utah Catholics to marshal their spiritual resources: "Under the circumstances, it is our patriotic as well as religious duty to draw, in fullest possible measure, upon the spiritual and supernatural resources afforded us in our holy religion. I hereby direct, therefore, that on the day of invasion, the so-called "D" day, a Holy Hour be held in each church beginning at 7:30 in the evening, and this without further notice. I direct, also, that on each succeeding day, other fitting devotions be held, these to be continued until the crisis is safely passed."[23] Not surprisingly, then, at war's end, Bishop Hunt ordered a special celebration of gratitude to God for victory: "When the official announcement of V-J Day is made the Blessed Sacrament will be exposed immediately if the announcement is made in the daytime. If not, the Exposition will take place the following day, and will conclude with a Holy Hour in the evening at 7:30."[24]

As we have seen, Bishop Hunt suffered from weak eyesight most of his life, an affliction that forced him to drop out of law school. As his years as bishop wore on, his vision continued to fail, confining him more and more to his living quarters at Holy Cross Hospital, where youths he had befriended came to read to him.[25] In 1948 it became advisable for him to request an Auxiliary Bishop to take over diocesan ministries that he could now carry out only with great difficulty. It was a milestone in the history of the Cathedral when the newly consecrated Bishop Leo J. Steck came from St. Louis to take up his duties as the first Auxiliary in the history of the Church in Utah. Unfortunately, things did not work out as planned.

Born in St. Louis to George and Mathilda Steck, Leo Steck had first studied at St. Louis Preparatory Seminary and then at Kenrick Seminary, where he was ordained in 1924 by Cardinal John Glennon of St. Louis. He served as assistant at St. Peter's parish in Kirkwood, Missouri and in various other positions throughout the archdiocese before being appointed pastor of the Church of St. Gabriel the Archangel, where he received his call to Salt Lake City. Archbishop Ritter and Bishop Cody, both of St. Louis, along with Bishop Carroll of Wichita, co-consecrated him in the Cathedral of St. Louis on May 20, 1948, with Bishop Hunt delivering the sermon. Bishop Steck chose as his motto, "Not to be Ministered to, but to Minister." His ministry, however, barely got started before he became seriously ill. Only a year after his consecration, while on a fund-raising trip to St. Louis to raise money for his new diocese, Bishop Steck suffered a stroke. Initially thought to be not serious, the stroke nevertheless kept the bishop in the hospital for several months before his untimely death on June 19, 1950. Thus Bishop Hunt outlived his presumed successor.

Bishop Hunt's infirmity nevertheless continued, so another Auxiliary Bishop was appointed in 1951. This was Joseph Lennox Federal, a North Carolinian who then became Coadjutor Bishop in 1958, anticipating his succession to the episcopal throne. Bishop Hunt lingered on in life for another decade after Bishop Steck's death, finally succumbing to a heart problem on March 31, 1960.

Fig. 24: Working on Cathedral spire.

Chapter 4

Restoration

"Son of man, can these bones live?" (Ezekiel 37:3)

Joseph Lennox Federal, sixth bishop of the Diocese of Salt Lake City, was born in Greensboro, North Carolina, on January 13, 1910, the third of eight children, one of whom became a nun. During high school, at a boarding school run by the Benedictines, he began to feel a call to the priesthood, a vocation that was encouraged by an uncle who was a Vincentian priest. He studied at Belmont Abbey College in North Carolina and at Niagara University in New York (which granted him an honorary degree in 1951). After two years at the latter institution, he told his bishop of his desire to study for the priesthood, and he left the university to continue his studies at The Albertinium, the University of Fribourg, and the North American College in Rome (the "House on Humility Street," as it is called) prior to his ordination in Rome in 1934.

Upon returning home, his first assignment was as assistant pastor at St. Peter's in Greenville, after which he was given the pastorate of St. Margaret's church in Swannanoa, a rural parish where he ministered largely to sharecroppers. For those impoverished Southerners, the abolition of slavery had meant little in economic terms, for the dependency of plantation life had simply been replaced by the peonage of indebtedness, the hopelessness of which was only then, in the late 1930s, beginning to be mitigated in parts of the South by programs like the Tennessee Valley Authority and the Farm Security Administration. Although he rarely discussed that period during his later life, the future bishop obviously distinguished himself in those ministries for, to his surprise, he was asked in 1938 to become rector of Sacred Heart Cathedral in Raleigh. It must have been an intimidating assignment for one ordained barely three years previously, but he rose to the challenge and served in that capacity for thirteen years, being named a Monsignor in the process.

In 1951 Msgr. Federal was named Auxiliary Bishop of Salt Lake City, the first native North Carolinian to be elevated to the American hierarchy. He was only 42 years old.[1] (When Bishop Hunt appointed him pastor of the Cathedral parish and rector to succeed Bishop-elect Dwyer in 1952, Bishop Federal experienced the rare honor of serving as pastor of the cathedral parishes of two diocese within two years.) Interestingly, it was none other than Bishop Hunt who gave the sermon at the ordination Mass. He had been in Florida recovering from an illness when he received word of the appointment. At the news, he expressed "profound gratitude to the Holy See and its consideration of the needs of the Salt Lake Diocese in assigning as aide a man who is himself thoroughly acquainted with the problems and difficulties confronting the church in a missionary area."[2] Monsignor Dwyer echoed the appropriateness of the appointment, noting that the new bishop was "himself intimately acquainted with the problems of the church in missionary America. There are few areas within the continental limits of the nation where the church is less broadly established than in our Diocese of Salt Lake, but it so happens that the Diocese of Raleigh is one of them." He went on to note that the 22,000 Catholics within the 4,000,000 population of North Carolina was even a much thinner percentage than the 25,000 Catholics in Utah's almost 689,000.[3]

Bishop Federal became an enthusiastic adopted son of Utah, a fact he later underscored by choosing to spend his retirement here rather than returning to his native state. In 1958 he was named Coadjuter Bishop, anticipating his succession to Bishop Duane G. Hunt, which in fact occurred in 1960.

From the heights of the Cathedral which Bishop Federal inherited from Bishop Hunt one could view a vastly different scene from that which had greeted Bishop Scanlan. The dirt roads the pioneer priests traveled had evolved into pavement that pushed its way hungrily in every direction

Fig. 25: Bishop Federal inspects the new pinnacles.

out across the state. A growing populace and an industrialized, capitalistic economy required the increased mobility of freeways. A noxious smog, now caused by automotive exhaust, recalled the coal stove smoke of earlier days. And, there were even bigger changes on the way, changes that would rock the very foundations of the Catholic Church, yet propel it into the modern world.

One of the last acts of Pope Pius XII in 1958 was to appoint Bishop Federal coadjutor to Bishop Hunt. By the end of the year he was dead and when the white smoke ascended over St. Peter's Square, the world learned that his successor would be John XXIII, who became one of the most beloved popes in history, but one who brought about some of the most far-reaching changes in church history, changes that the new Bishop Federal would have to implement in the Diocese of Salt Lake City.

In September 1962 Bishop Federal sailed from New York City to Rome on the *Leonardo da Vinci* for the formal opening of the Second Vatican Council on October 11. He would eventually attend all four sessions of the council in successive years. Even those who attended could hardly have understood the magnitude of the changes they were igniting, for they would fundamentally change the liturgy of the Mass, the role of the laity, the relationship of the Church to other faiths and the rest of the world, and many other things that most Catholics thought would remain eternally unaltered.

Fig. 26: Msgr. William H. McDougall, Cathedral rector (L), watches the installation of a capstone.

If anyone doubts that God has a sense of humor, he should reflect upon the irony of the fact that it was Bishop Federal who had to assume the responsibility for implementing the changes mandated by the Council. Deeply conservative in his own nature and steeped in the genteel aristocratic culture of the South, he struggled with the rapid and sweeping changes initiated by the Council, while yet recognizing the potential for good in those changes and gradually allowing them to take root in the diocese.

The most difficult was the *Constitution on the Sacred Liturgy*, which was promulgated on December 4, 1963 and whose changes proved to be unsettling to some. In June, at the invitation of the Council of Churches of Salt Lake City, Bishop Federal spoke before 800 people in the Union Building of the University of Utah as part of his program of clarifying the Church's teachings for both the Catholic and non-Catholic communities and of guiding his people through the confusion of their spiritual crisis.

All the fear and frustration that normally accompany significant change were unleashed within the Church as it worked its way through its mandated confrontation with modern life. Gradually over the following decade, many of the changes decreed by the council became reality. The new order of Mass replaced one four centuries old; the priest-celebrant, formerly intoning the Latin liturgy alone at the altar, seemingly separated from the people, now led the worship in a manner involving the people themselves. On September 12, 1965, the first Mass in English was offered in the Cathedral by Father Patrick R. McInally. Baptisms, weddings, funerals, and the reformed Rite of Reconciliation were performed according to revised rituals which invited full participation of those around whom the liturgy centered: the parents, the bride and groom, the family of the deceased, the penitent. In 1967 acoustic guitars were approved for use in the liturgy "no more than once a week" in the Cathedral.[4] Some of the liturgical changes such as the Sign of Peace and Communion in the hand, first distributed in the Cathedral in October 1977, proved especially painful for some Catholics at the outset. As the diocesan newspaper reported after two years' experience with the changes, "explanations and time and personal experience with them generally won over most, although a significant, articulate minority continue to find those developments distressing."[5]

Fig. 27: Crane and scaffolding on the South Temple side of the Cathedral.

The other major issue facing Bishop Federal concerned the Cathedral building itself. The Cathedral throne maintains that continuity of Christianity prophesied and recorded in the Canon of the Mass: "From age to age He gathers a people unto Himself." The Cathedral building itself expresses this tradition of faith. It has been called both a museum of the past and a mosaic of the present. Though only a microcosm of the worldwide

Church, it had stood for seventy years as the local reminder of that ancient and worldwide heritage. In April 1970 the Cathedral was declared an official Historical Site by the Utah State Historical Society, and the following year it was listed on the National Register of Historic Places. A 15 x 19 inch bronze plaque impervious to weathering was mounted on the stone at the left side of the entrance to the steps of the Cathedral.

But all was not well. The physical structure of the Cathedral, long subjected to a slow, insidious deterioration by the city's weather extremes, began feeling the weight of its years. As early as the late 1940s, when some minor exterior repairs were accomplished, it was apparent that the annual freeze-thaw cycle and the increase of industrial pollutants in the valley had eroded the exterior sandstone. The first cleaning of the complete exterior of the Cathedral had been undertaken in January 1959 by sandblasters elevated to the top of the 150-foot towers in bosun's chairs. In the fall of 1960, major roof repairs were undertaken to protect the interior plaster with its priceless murals. Repairs were also carried out on the louvres in the fleche that rises from the north portion of the church by the Jay Olsen Company.

Despite these repairs, though, erosion continued its destructive work, and by 1975 the sandstone on the two towers and the façade, as well as the roof, appeared badly worn. The need for action to preserve the historic structure was discussed from time to time, but it was the sudden plunge of a sixty-pound piece of sandstone, the size of a watermelon, down from the heights of the Cathedral towers that set in motion the long-contemplated restoration process. The falling stone was deflected, but not until it had torn up a plank in its path and gutted a hole in the three-quarter inch plywood roof. Emergency measures with swing lifts were taken to remove other chunks of stone and slate that had broken loose and perched in dangerously precarious positions. The basic structural integrity of the building, fortunately, was deemed to be sound.

Less fortunate was the fact that the diocese and the Cathedral parish had had enough financial difficulties over the years that no endowment or other funds had been created to support the needed renovation, so a fund drive had to be launched. Accordingly, Bishop Federal announced the million-dollar Cathedral Restoration Drive, the largest financial campaign in the history of the Cathedral to that time. "The building, maintenance and restoration of churches, is a vital part of the Christian apostolate," Msgr. Francis J. Weber, archivist of the Archdiocese of Los Angeles pointed out, referring to the tumultuous decade in which the restoration was accomplished. "Surely no society in all of recorded history needs points of repose and rest, places of silence and peace or centers of worship and community more than does that of the 1970's."[6]

In the Cathedral restoration, as well as in all other aspects of Cathedral life, Bishop Federal was fortunate to have the assistance of Msgr. William H. McDougall, Jr. (1909–1988), who had been ordained at the Cathedral in 1952 and became rector in the 1960s. Born in Salt Lake City, McDougall grew up in a house almost directly across the street from Our Lady of Lourdes parish, of which his mother was a long-time member of the Altar Society. As a young man, he developed an impressive reputation as a reporter for the *Salt Lake Telegram*. On the eve of World War II, he quit his job, traveled to Japan, and went to work on an English language newspaper there. From there he moved to Shanghai as a correspondent for the United Press. He covered the Japanese invasion of the Netherlands East Indies (Indonesia), but the ship on which he was making his escape was sunk, and he spent an anxious three hours floating in the sea before being picked up by a life boat. Although the boat made it to a landing on Sumatra, McDougall, along with its occupants, was captured and spent the rest of the war in Japanese prison camps.

Although the journals he kept during his internment do not indicate a dramatic spiritual transformation, such a conversion nevertheless took place gradually, from a rather casual Catholic into a vocation to the priesthood. After his ordination, McDougall devoted his journalistic skills to the *Intermountain Catholic*, and as rector of the Cathedral, he exhibited a deep interest in the building's history and welfare. Never in good health after his incarceration, he was known for his devotion to the poor and homeless.[7]

In May and June 1975 workers erected scaffolding around the front and west sides of the building. The work began at the top, where the need was most urgent, and proceeded downwards. Erosion was most critical on the west spire and work began there in July. The sandstone used in the building had originally been quarried in 1900 from Carbon County. Sandstone had been chosen rather than granite, presumably, because of

the excessively high cost of granite. Being porous, sandstone collects moisture
which freezes in the winter, expanding
and cracking the stone.

Precast stone, a mixture of concrete
and reinforcing materials, was chosen
for the outside repairs because it is less
expensive than sandstone and three to
four times as strong, though it is more
difficult to work with because it has to
be mixed and poured within a short period of time. Both in color and texture
it blends well with the natural sandstone. Locating stone masons qualified
for this kind of work proved impos-
sible locally, so the general contractor,
Devcon Industries, Inc., brought in three masons from New York.

Fig. 28: Bishop Federal supervising
the Cathedral restoration.

Using huge cranes, workers removed the eroded sandstone pieces from
the towers and lowered them to trucks for disposal, then replaced them with
the reinforced concrete. The new stones were cast in fiberglass molds. An
epoxy mortar was used to hold them in place. On the east tower a section of
stone was found to be so seriously eroded and so extensive in size that its repair cost $300,000 more than anticipated for that phase of the restoration.

One difficult problem involved the finials, the ornamental caps on
the Cathedral pinnacles. The original ones were stone, but they had been
replaced with copper ones, probably in the 1930s. Although they could
last indefinitely, they had to be removed in order to replace the stones
beneath them, and it was decided at that time to replace them with stone
ones resembling the originals. It was a challenging operation to lift the
eight seven-ton caps, each ten feet high, into place on top of the towers.
(The west tower measures 180 feet from the ground, and because of the
slope in the land, the east tower measures 160 feet; they are equal in alti-
tude, but not in distance above the ground.) It took Style Crete, Inc., the
subcontractor for the finials, some four months to build them. Although
the original stone finials had been fashioned of stones of different hues,

architects and specialists decided to use a uniform buff color for the new ones to match dominant tones elsewhere on the building.

Work proceeded onto the roof, where the old slate was replaced with copper, starting on the north end. An unanticipated problem was that the steel roof trusses needed reinforcement, and old nuts and bolts which had rusted had to be replaced.

Gargoyles were not included in the exterior façade of the original Cathedral, but they were installed as part of the 1917 renovation. Like gargoyles on medieval cathedrals, they were used as rainspouts, making an impressive display as water gushed from their mouths during a storm. But that water had an erosive effect on the stone figures, and by 1930, nothing was left of the gargoyles. Eight new gargoyles were designed by Peter Cole, an art student at the University of Utah. Working from a full-sized clay model sculpted by Cole, Style Crete, Inc. created a mold from which the new figures were cast. They are buff in color and highly resistant to erosion. Designed in the Gothic style, they appear to be a petrified cross among a bird, a dog, and a cat. A huge crane with a 240-foot boom blocked half of South Temple Street for several days in September 1977 while crews hoisted the monsters, each weighing 1,200 pounds, to the 150-foot level of the tower tops, four on the east and four on the west tower. These gargoyles do not serve as rainspouts, channeling water out and away from the walls as in traditional Gothic cathedrals, but are strictly ornamental, nevertheless adding an authentic Gothic element to the architecture.

The Cathedral's stained glass windows were originally set in wooden frames, but over time the wood had badly rotted, threatening destruction to the windows. In 1957 a new framework cast of Buehner "Mo-sai" concrete, in a texture and color that harmonized perfectly with the sandstone walls, was installed around the rose window and the transept windows. Now, in the 1970s, the framework around the nave windows was replaced with the precast stone which similarly blended in hue and texture with the Cathedral walls.

As the work proceeded, scaffolding slowly receded from the heights of the Cathedral and concentrated on stonework at lower levels. Stone trimwork, some of it highly decorative, was recast and placed during 1978 and

Fig. 29: One of the newly installed gargoyles.

1979. The sound of pneumatic tools reshaping sandstone blocks became a familiar one around the Cathedral.

Work on the interior began. There was no intention to modernize nor renovate, simply to clean the painted surfaces, restoring the original colors, and to polish and clean the woodwork. That, too, turned out to be more of a job than anticipated, as it was learned that the leaky original roof had allowed water to spoil some of the plaster around the arches and in the ceiling.

The front doors were also refinished. The original plan was to repair and refinish others of the exquisite woodwork and carvings within the Cathedral, a project for which the services of expert artisans would be solicited. But as the unanticipated extent and cost overruns of exterior essentials developed, the completion of these interior proposals were placed in doubt.

The lights in Bishop Scanlan's Cathedral were attached to the pillars along the side aisles. In 1917 Bishop Glass installed lights hanging from the ceiling. The 1977 restoration work increased the candlepower of those lights and added spotlights directed toward and accentuating the intricacies

Fig. 30: Msgr. William H. McDougall celebrating Mass at the portable post-Vatican II altar.

of the stained glass windows, hand-carved wooden figures and murals. This new lighting system, which made the vaulting much more visible, was designed by the Rambusch Company of New York, which had contracted the lighting system for Bishop Glass in 1917 also.

The acoustical properties of the Cathedral have always been problematic. In an attempt to make sound more clearly and uniformly audible, speakers were positioned in an opening in the ceiling in the nave directly above the center of the altar rail. The installation required the erection of scaffolding in the area and extending up into the sanctuary. The portable altar was moved aside and weekday services disrupted. Debris drifted down from the gaping hole atop the scaffolding, seemingly a final profane desecration of the sanctuary and symbolic of all the frustration that had accompanied the intrusive tools and trucks and cement mixers and piles of sand and gravel and all the trappings of reconstruction and repair over the previous five years. When the interior scaffolding finally disappeared and the Cathedral could return to order on November 30, 1979, it hopefully presaged a permanent return to peace.

The wooden construction barriers at the B Street court were removed by early 1980. New basement doors were installed. Meeting rooms and classrooms were completed in the basement by April. A new heating system was installed and the entire basement painted. Throughout the building and grounds, repair equipment slowly retreated and order was restored.

In February the Cathedral sanctuary, for the first time in its history, became the setting for a dramatic production. The Cathedral Playmakers staged a production of "Damien," directed by Robert Bruce Smith and starring actor Dan Rogers. Paradoxically, what had been called a "fading baroque splendor" (now that it had stood the better part of a century) here found a fresh avenue of inspiration and utility. This new role and extended use somehow helped expand the vision of the Cathedral into contemporary need, and opened the door for it to become the center for various arts performances that it became under Bishop Weigand. It became more a sermon in stone speaking to the major concerns of the day.

On a darker note, the Cathedral is subject to the tensions of the times. Vandalism occurs occasionally. Early in 1980, for example, thieves broke a stained glass window in the sacristy to enter the sanctuary, presumably to search for items of value, but were deterred by burglar alarms. On April 2, 1980, Sexton Jan Scholte arrived early in the morning to find one of the small windows in the newly finished front doors smashed and glass splattered on the entrance steps.

The funds for the restoration project had, by the end of five years, become nearly depleted. Bishop Federal had launched the Cathedral Restoration Drive on "Action Sunday," May 18, 1975 to solicit from the total Catholic community $800,000 of a $1,000,000 goal. By May 30, $901,000 had been pledged in a generous response that expressed the love and appreciation of the people for their bishop and his Cathedral. Two area families gave $50,000 each and one $25,000; a business firm donated $35,000, all remaining anonymous. Non-Catholics, recognizing the historical and cultural importance of the Cathedral added to those sums, as did the business community of the city. From the National Park Service funds appropriated in 1975 through the National Historic Preservation Act, the project received $56,250. An additional $37,000 from the same source was obtained through the mediation of the Utah State Historical Society. This last sum was temporarily jeopardized by an objection from the Heritage Conservation and Recreation Service of the Department of the Interior over the use of copper for the new roof instead of slate, but the Historical Society submitted a justification for the change on the basis of the fact that copper was a superior material to protect from the leaks historically experienced with slate and the grant was made in January 1979. By July the bishop announced that $1,039,179 had been raised, and he proposed a budget for the projected renovations. Once the work was begun, however, it was found that actual costs and unanticipated needs depleted the funds to a point where only essential work could be completed.

Among the unexpected expenses were those arising out of a fire that broke out on Saturday, May 19, 1979. Fortunately the fire was noticed in time by roofers who were still at work and by passersby, for fire fighters estimated that if it had burned unchecked for another ten or fifteen minutes, the copper roof would have been ruined. One fortunate result of the fire was the installation of fire detection devices which, though expensive, were necessary lest another such fire break out in the night with much more serious consequences.

The restoration program could not be considered complete until the interior work was carried out as planned. But Bishop Federal felt forced to leave to his successor that phase of the project. In view of the exertion of the fundraising effort and the disruption and frustration of the construction work and the cost overruns, it was perhaps enough for one bishop to have accomplished.

Once he reached the age of seventy, and mindful of the Second Vatican Council recommendation that bishops resign once they perceive that their work was being impaired by the infirmities of age, Bishop Federal retired. Pope John Paul II accepted his resignation on April 22, 1980. The following months were a time of farewells, while Bishop Federal continued to conduct the affairs of the diocese as Apostolic Administrator until his successor was appointed on September 3, 1980. Some 800 friends and admirers attended a retirement banquet at the Hotel Utah, enthusiastically agreeing with banquet speaker John W. Gallivan, who predicted that "When the history of the Diocese of Salt Lake is written, the chapter entitled 'The Federal Years' will triumphantly glow."[8]

Fig. 31: Scaffolding fills the upper level of the Cathedral during the 1991–93 renovation.

Chapter 5

Renovation

"Day and night, without pause, they sing,
'Holy, holy, holy is the Lord God Almighty'" (Revelation 4:8).

With Bishop Federal's retirement, the diocese next passed into the hands of a forty-three-year-old priest from Homedale, Idaho. William K. Weigand was born in Bend, Oregon, on May 23, 1937 to Harold J. and Alice P. Kennedy Weigand. After studies at Mount Angel Minor Seminary, Saint Benedict, Oregon, and Saint Thomas Seminary in Kenmore, Washington, he was ordained May 25, 1963 at St. Mary's Church in St. Maries, Idaho. He served in various capacities in the Diocese of Boise before departing for Cali, Colombia, in 1968, where he was appointed to serve in San Juan Bautista parish, an Idaho mission, for three years, but he became so enthusiastic and engaged in the assignment that it stretched to nine years. Upon his return to the United States in December 1977, he was assigned to St. Hubert's parish in Homedale, where he was serving when called to the Diocese of Salt Lake City.[1]

His ordination took place before a capacity congregation in the Salt Palace on the evening of Monday, November 17, 1980. Addressing the people fluently in both English and Spanish, the new bishop indicated his determination to reach out to the alienated and the disadvantaged in all walks of life and racial origins. He acknowledged that his freedom to do so was made possible by Bishop Federal's "tireless dedication to addressing the fundamental physical and organization[al] needs of a growing diocese."[2] Bishop

Fig. 32: A relic of an earlier time: the names of pew renters remained on the pews until the 1990s renovation, during which the pews were refinished.

Weigand spent the first weeks of his episcopacy meeting the clergy, religious and laity of his diocese in a series of pastoral seminars, before undertaking the visitation of the various parishes throughout his far-flung diocese.

The new bishop's coat of arms was rich in symbolism and prophetic of the course his ministry would take. His episcopal motto, "Feed My Lambs," emphasized his focus on those searching for the good news of the Gospel. In particular, the field upon which the other symbols rested represented building blocks which symbolize building up the church community, It was a prophetic symbol in view of the fact that a good part of his tenure would be devoted to the $10.4 million interior renovation of the Cathedral.[3]

What sort of man now occupied Salt Lake City's episcopal throne? Personally shy and often diffident in the presence of strangers, he was nevertheless a hard-driving worker and a challenging leader. A person of monkishly simple tastes, he drove a battered Volkswagen Rabbit and lived in a small house in a largely Hispanic neighborhood on Salt Lake City's west side, where he grew some of his own food in a backyard garden. His infrequent holidays and vacations were often spent visiting his mother or fishing with one or another of his priests. His years in Colombia (where, incidentally, he recruited a number of priests and seminarians for the Salt Lake City diocese) had exerted an obviously profound influence on him, shown in his deep love for Hispanic people and the Spanish language. Bishop Weigand spoke Spanish with a fluency that often exceeded that of native speakers, whose grammar he would occasionally correct. His homilies at Mass, which could sometimes become lengthy and digressive, almost always included a section in Spanish. In a diocese where the number of Spanish-speaking members was rapidly increasing, his linguistic fluency was an invaluable pastoral asset.

Unknown to most in the diocese, Bishop Weigand was increasingly ill during his last years in Salt Lake City, an illness he bore with stoical self-denial. The true dimensions of his suffering never emerged until he became Bishop of Sacramento, when his health failed so badly that he had to have a liver transplant.[4]

Once installed in the Diocese of Salt Lake City, the new bishop found one project already on the docket: completion of the restoration of the Cathedral. The massive restoration, which Bishop Weigand put into motion in 1987, was the most expensive and ambitious project of his tenure in Salt Lake City. In 1986, Bishop Weigand appointed Fr. M. Francis Mannion as rector of the Cathedral. The appointment of Fr. Mannion, who had just completed a Ph.D. in sacramental theology at The Catholic University of America, marked the beginning of a new phase of liturgical life in the Cathedral, as well as a new prominence for the Cathedral in the civic, artistic and cultural life of the community, including such programs as the Madeleine Festival of the Arts and Humanities, the Eccles Organ Festival, the Madeleine Choir School, the (later discontinued) McDougall Lectures, and a vastly expanded Good Samaritan Program. The renovation project was scheduled to recognize the centennial of the Diocese of Salt Lake City in 1991 and the Cathedral's historical significance as a state and national monument and a symbol of spiritual strength for people of all faiths.

Facing a daunting task of such massive scope, Bishop Weigand worked closely with a small steering committee (the Architectural Planning Committee) comprised of Fr. Mannion, Richard Howa, M. Ray Kingston, and Irene Sweeney to nurture the project in all its architectural and fund-raising aspects. Although Bishop Weigand was the active director and chief fund-raiser, he called upon the generous assistance of four co-chairmen, John W. Gallivan, Jon M. Huntsman, Sr., Ian M. Cumming, and Richard Keiffer. The fact that only one of the four (Gallivan) was a Catholic is a significant symbol of the bishop's attempt to make the Cathedral renovation a community project rather than just a Catholic one.

Father (later Monsignor) Mannion, Cathedral rector and recognized liturgical scholar, served as the project manager and campaign moderator, guiding seemingly endless stages of planning and the work of steering committees studying the feasibility of a financial projection of $6.3 million, as well as organizational charts, strategies, timetables, special events, and architectural proposals.[5] At the height of the project, Msgr. Mannion was regularly putting in fourteen hour days on the renovation alone, in an involvement so intense that people sometimes apologized for bringing pastoral matters to his attention. "I'd become a renovation bureaucrat for a number of years," he recalled.[6]

At the point where the size of the project and its financial scope began to come into focus (though both grew dramatically as time passed), fundraising consultant John B. Cummings of Dallas was hired to conduct a feasibility study. It was obvious that the relatively small Catholic community was not going to be able to muster all the necessary funds, so Cummings's role was to determine whether the project could be sold to the community at large as well. His study revealed that it could, largely because the outside community had already come to recognize the Cathedral not only as an important architectural landmark, but also as an important center of cultural diversity, artistic performance, and charitable activity. "If you want to gain public financial support for your church renovations, your church must be a public church," Msgr. Mannion observed.[7]

Since the project was going to be sold to non-Catholics as a community enterprise rather than just a Catholic one, a separately endowed entity called the Cathedral Preservation Fund was created to receive funds for the renovation. That fund, which had a board of directors, about half of whom were not Catholics, enabled donors to contribute to the project rather than to the church.

Cummings had been retained by the Cathedral largely because he was under no illusions about the difficulty of rais-ing renovation funds within the unique

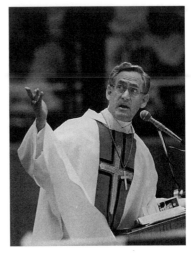

Fig. 33: Bishop William K. Weigand.

demographic and culture of Salt Lake City. He was kept as fund-raising consultant because his firm was a small one that undertook no more than three projects at once, so he could give close personal attention to this one. That was especially important because neither Bishop Weigand nor Msgr. Mannion had had any fund-raising experience. In the end, though, fund-raising firms do not raise funds; that has to be done by local project leaders who are instructed by the consultant as to who to approach and how to approach them. The leader in this case, of course, was Bishop Weigand. At first, his shyness made fund-raising difficult, but Msgr. Mannion remembers that "in the beginning he was very shy about doing that, and very quickly he got very good at it."[8] Bishop Weigand had the constant support of Miss Irene Sweeney, treasurer of the Cathedral Preservation Fund, and one of the major donors to the renovation project.

The New York City architectural firm of Beyer Blinder Belle was chosen to design the renovation. The firm had extensive experience in historic preservation projects like Ellis Island and Grand Central Station, as well as renovation of the art in several state capitols. John Belle was the partner in charge of this project. James Fitch, director of historic preservation for the firm and one of the fathers of historic preservation in the United States, was in his eighties at the time, yet he took a personal interest in the project and flew out to Salt Lake City every time the architects came, in order to oversee the work. Perhaps the most conspicuous elements in the

Fig. 34: Gregory Glenn playing the organ at the hard hat party before closing the Cathedral.

renovation—the altar and the Blessed Sacrament chapel with its screen and tabernacle—were designed by a woman, Norma Barbacci, probably the only woman ever involved in the development of liturgical elements in a cathedral in this country.[9]

Beyer Blinder Belle presented their plans for the schematic design phase of the work at the restoration inauguration reception on October 11, 1989.[10] During the same year, seminars in the regional deaneries of the diocese coordinated by Msgr. Mannion energized parishioners' support as the restoration slowly took on momentum. By 1991 a major diocesan and statewide campaign exceeded its goal by raising $6,380,721 in pledges. Like Bishop Federal's earlier restoration project, however, this one also encountered unforeseen expenses, this time in the form of a seismic retrofit of the tower, roof, and walls, the need for which became apparent after the devastating 1990 earthquakes in San Francisco. That added an additional unexpected $1.8 million to the already staggering costs.[11] This time, though, the more effective fund-raising efforts directed by John B. Cummings and put into action by Bishop Weigand and Msgr. Mannion tapped into a deep wellspring of community support so that incoming monies kept exceeding the project's costs. When that happened, the ambitious and creative Bishop Weigand would suggest additional renovations. In that leapfrogging way, a $6.1 million project grew to a $10.4 million one.[12]

Another potential cost overrun involved a way to improve parking at the Cathedral, which has always been a problem. Besides parking on the streets, there were two lots on the Cathedral property itself: the upper lot on First Avenue, and the lower lot between the Cathedral and the Diocesan Pastoral Center. Bishop Weigand wanted to replace both lots with a parking garage, but Salt Lake City zoning officials would have none of that. Instead, a private donor came forth with an offer to pay for a large circular fountain that would turn the lower lot into a quiet plaza while hardly diminishing the available parking. So the Cathedral received a certain external beautification as part of the renovation, and at no cost to the project.[13]

At last a Hard Hat party, staged in the nave of the Cathedral in 1991, launched the actual construction phase that would possess the interior for two years. On February 20, 1991, the structure was closed and a local construction company, Culp Construction, went to work, raising scaffolding, hauling out pews for refinishing, removing the stained glass windows for reconstruction, and soon falling plaster and sawdust littered the floor. It was an exciting enterprise, but a frightening one as well. Both Msgr. Mannion and Choir School founder Gregory Glenn remember how their hearts used to fall when they walked into the gutted building. "The ceiling was pulled down, the walls were pulled out, the floor was pulled up, everything looked like a bomb site," Msgr. Mannion recalled. "Sometimes I used to say to myself, 'Can we ever get it back together again?'" Glenn remembered saying to Msgr. Mannion, "I think this may be a huge mistake."[14]

For the next two years, Cathedral Masses were celebrated at Lowell School, a nearby elementary school which the parish was able to rent on weekends. Although some Cathedral parishioners endured the move with a sense of humor, dubbing the place "St. Lowell," others decided to spend their exile at other parish churches. Since about sixty percent of Cathedral parishioners actually reside within other parish boundaries, there was a serious risk of desertion. To help counteract that, the renovation team designed lapel buttons which they wore at Lowell proclaiming their commitment to staying. Gregory Glenn remembered that it was difficult even to hold the Cathedral choir together: "It was easy to attract members to sing in a neo-Gothic building, but it was not so easy to attract them to sing in a basketball gymnasium" accompanied only by a beat-up upright piano. But he also recalled that even that adversity had a positive dimension: "It was an opportunity for us to reflect on things and do some planning for moving back into the Cathedral. So it was a good time of intensive work, preparation, building up repertoire, figuring out a pattern for how things were going to develop. We used that to our best advantage."[15]

One of the biggest parts of the project was restoration—indeed, "reconstruction" would not be too vigorous a word—of the twenty-one stained glass windows, which was accomplished by Rohlf's Stained and Leaded

Fig. 35: Re-installing a Cathedral window.

Glass studio in Mount Vernon, New York. The windows were in a seriously, even dangerously, deteriorated condition. One of the problems was that the F. X. Zettler firm which had created the windows had used a grade of lead that was not long-lasting in which to set the glass pieces, so that over time the windows had loosened. That problem was exacerbated by the fact that during the Bishop Federal restoration, clear panes of glass had been placed over the outside of the window openings to protect the stained glass, but no ventilation openings had been provided. The result was that the space between the two panes would become extremely hot during the summer, causing further deterioration of the lead. By the time they were removed the windows exhibited an alarming degree of buckling. In fact, during the process of removing the Presentation of the Child Jesus window, the window gave way and plunged into the ground. What seemed a catastrophe in the end turned out all right. The restorers had to dismantle completely each window anyway to replace the lead and some inferior panes of glass which had been used in various repair operations over the years, so they were able to rebuild the dropped one. "And it was rebuilt so expertly that it actually looked better than the original," observed Msgr. Mannion. When the windows were reinstalled, a venting system was provided.[16]

Makeshift elevators, one in the interior and one outside, lifted art restorationists from Evergreene Paint Studios of New York onto high platforms to restore the Cathedral's originally magnificent murals from erosion and water damage as well as to remove the canvas sagging from the walls and to prevent the threat of falling plaster that had chipped away. During the initial planning of the renovation, Cathedral parishioners had been shocked when Msgr. Mannion asked that a small section of paint on the wall near the bishop's chair to be cleaned of the accumulated grime of air pollution and incense smoke. The vivid colors beneath the filth were dazzling, and one could only imagine what the Cathedral would look like when everything had been cleaned. Elsewhere in the interior, woodcarvers and finishers repaired and refinished statues, paneling, the ambo, and ornate reredos behind the high altar and side chapels. Working beside them were lighting and acoustical engineers, carpenters reconfiguring pews and confessionals, artisans constructing sections of new tile flooring, and an artist, Roger "Sam" Wilson of the University of Utah, completing a new set of Stations of the Cross.

The Stations of the Cross in Bishop Scanlan's Cathedral were white bas relief sculptures, but they had been replaced during Bishop Glass's renovation with oil paintings of a rather gloomy nature in Renaissance style. The desirability of replacing them became a necessity: when cleaned, they looked even murkier than before, and when removed from the frames, they simply fell apart. In an attempt to find an artist who could execute new Stations, a Liturgy Committee headed by Msgr. Mannion conducted a national search, but none of the samples submitted seemed satisfactory. Then someone suggested Sam Wilson at the University, and when Msgr. Mannion visited him and inspected his work, he was impressed. Wilson received the commission, and the fact that he was not a Catholic only supported the point that the Cathedral renovation was a community project, not just a Catholic one.

Although a committee was appointed for each one of the Stations, to do research and suggest elements that might be included, the Liturgy Committee repeatedly emphasized that the committees were only doing their work in a supportive role, and the ultimate design was to be Wilson's alone. The actual subjects of the Stations were another matter, and the Liturgy Committee decided to abandon some of the traditional scenes

Fig. 36: Roger "Sam" Wilson and one of his Stations of the Cross.

that had no Biblical base — Veronica Wiping the Brow of Jesus, for example — in favor of ones that did. In the end, Wilson's rendition of the
Stations turned out to be the one element in the Cathedral renovation that
could be considered somewhat novel. They are so complex, with each one
containing several figures, and loaded with symbolism, that a brochure
had to be created to enable viewers to interpret what they were seeing.[17]

One unforeseen element in the renovation was the moving of the remains of Bishop Scanlan, which had been interred in a basement room of
the Cathedral. The immense weight of the new altar and chancel had to
be supported by new pillars reaching into the basement, and the necessary
placement of one was through the room where the sepulcher was located.
Gregory Glenn, the Cathedral's newest staff member who had just transferred over from the Diocesan Office of Liturgy, was appointed to oversee
the removal of the remains.

As things turned out, it was a fortunate opportunity, because the room
was not a very noble place to leave a bishop's remains: it was crooked and
cramped (Deacon Lynn Johnson, a professional photographer, remembered

that in order to get onto the far side of the sepulcher to photograph the inscription, he had to clamber over the sepulcher itself). The Cathedral had never been planned as a bishop's tomb, so no place had been provided for such a thing. At the time of the dedication of the Cathedral in 1909, Cardinal James Gibbons of Baltimore had suggested to Bishop Scanlan that he should consider being interred there. Apparently it took a long time for the bishop to make up his mind on the matter, but it was his last request, and his executors then had to find whatever space was available.[18]

When Glenn arrived on the scene, morticians had removed the sarcophagus. The casket had almost completely disintegrated, but the bishop had not. It was a touching scene: "I remember he was inviolate," Glenn said. "His body was all present. His skin was there. He looked very much like a dried flower, that kind of appearance. He was all intact. He had his crozier and his mitre, the old pontifical sunburst gloves. His hands were folded. He was a very tall man, very tall. That was a very striking moment." Funeral home director Neil O'Donnell donated a new casket and stored the bishop's remains for the entire two-year renovation period while a new place was provided for the sepulcher upstairs behind the old high altar. Then, during the rededication ceremony in 1993, a solemn procession brought the remains upstairs to their ultimate resting place. "So our great founder is now with us in the upper church," Glenn pointed out, "and that's good."[19]

The central focus of the interior of the church was the altar, fashioned, like the new baptismal font, of Carrara onyx and glass mosaic and situated on a marble chancel at the intersection of the nave and transept. Pews on either side of the chancel were turned to face east and west toward the altar in accordance with liturgical renewal provisions in order to promote the idea of the Eucharist as a communal meal. The altar's centrality is further emphasized by four new chandeliers designed by Roger Morgan of New York and situated roughly over the four candlesticks surrounding the altar. The optical effect is to make the altar appear larger than it actually is.

Other interior alterations included moving the bishop's chair, or cathedra (no longer to be referred to as a throne, in the general changes of the post-Vatican II Church) from the west side of the sanctuary to a central position behind the altar. This presented a problem of where to situate the tabernacle which, like the bishop's chair, should be along the central axis of the church. A way to do this without having the two elements competing for visual attention with each other was suggested during a brief visit by liturgical consultant Murray McCance, who pointed out that a latticework screen could be erected behind the bishop's chair to create a Blessed Sacrament chapel in which the tabernacle would be the central element, with seats and kneelers for private prayer. The latticework enables the tabernacle to be seen from the church proper, while yet occupying its own sacred space. The fourteen-foot high tabernacle was created by Master carver Ian Agrell of Agrell and Thorpe in California, as well as the twenty-two foot wide chancel screen.

In the space vacated by the bishop's chair was installed a Bishops' Memorial, giving the names, birthplaces, and vital dates of each of the bishops of the diocese. The bishop's chair itself, as well as cushions in the Blessed Sacrament chapel, were decorated in a volunteer effort by the Utah Women's Needlework Guild. The ambo, or the pulpit from which the readings and the homily are given, was lowered by removing six of the original eight steps as designed in 1909. The two side chapels under the transept windows were rededicated to Our Lady of Guadalupe, patroness of the Americas, on the west (icon painted by Patrick Fiore of Florida), and Christ the Good Shepherd on the east (painted by Brother Claude Lane OSB, of Mount Angel Abbey in Oregon).

Visually complementing the altar at the other end of the nave as one enters the church from South Temple was an ornate octagonal baptismal font constructed of the same Carrara onyx and glass mosaic and symbolizing the "eighth day" of Creation (eternity) and the Cross. Its location just inside the church symbolizes that baptism is our entrance into the Church. The unit includes both an upper font for infant baptism and a lower font for adults, enabling a return to the ancient ritual of baptism by immersion. Since the unit is actually set into the floor, it presented the peril of inattentive people falling in, so a railing was installed around it in the spring of 2009.

The original baptistry was a separate room to the east of the main entrance to the Cathedral in which people both literally and symbolically "outside" the Church were baptized and then brought inside. In the renovation this was redesignated the Magdalen Room with installation of a statue of St. Mary Magdalen created in the 1940s by Canadian artist Gordon Newby, with two racks of votive candles. To the original

Fig. 37: Preparing the baptismal font for use during the Easter services.

eight stained glass windows were added two "Vatican II" windows com-memorating the ecumenical movement and the Church's commitment to dialogue with the modern world as set forth in the Council document *Lumen Gentium*. Finally, during the 1990s, a Madonna and Child statue of Portuguese rose marble carved in Italy in 1958 by Mormon sculptor Avard Fairbanks was donated by his son, Dr. Grant R. Fairbanks. An interesting feature of the Madonna is that she was rendered as a Mormon pioneer woman, with gnarly hands. Though a Mormon, Fairbanks seems to have had an accurate understanding of the role that art plays in Catholic churches. "The hope of the world lies in our faith and in our spiritual ideals," he wrote. "Such ideals we express in material form."[20] With the installation of the Fairbanks statue, the room was renamed the Our Lady of Zion chapel.

The original Cathedral had four confessionals, two at the rear of the church and two in the transepts. In this renovation, those in the transepts were removed and the ones at the rear enlarged to facilitate the face-to-face option for the Sacrament of Reconciliation provided for after the Second Vatican Council. On the east side of the Blessed Sacrament chapel is the ambry, a cabinet which holds the Holy Oils of Chrism, Oil of the Sick and the Oil of Catechumens in addition to the Cathedral's relic of the True Cross. The ambry was originally the sedilia, or the clergy's bench. High above South Temple Street, two new bells cast by the Verdin Company of Cincinnati and sounding the notes of B and C# were added to the Cathedral's two original ones at a total cost of almost $70,000.[21]

Finally, the Cathedral received a long-needed new organ. We have previously seen the problems that had developed with the original organ which had been donated by Miss Ellen Hayes of Ely, Nevada, at a cost of about $15,000 and renovated in 1951 by Monsignor Dwyer. By the mid-1980s, though, it had fallen into a state of deterioration again and simply could not justify another renovation. In addition, it was a strange combination of various organs and was not even adequate for liturgical accompaniment, let alone performance of standard organ literature, both church and classical.[22]

The new organ was designed and built specifically for the Cathedral by Kenneth Jones and Associates of Bray, Ireland, and paid for by a grant of one million dollars from the George S. and Dolores Doré Eccles Foundation.

Fig. 38: Preparing to install one of the new bells, named "Michael."

Spencer F. Eccles, acting for the Foundation, made the donation with the stipulation that the instrument could be used for liturgical purposes, but since the Foundation could not donate to churches, it also had to be used in public concerts and recitals as well.

Set in cases of solid oak matching the interior woodwork of the original Cathedral, the organ contains 4,066 pipes ranging in size from thirty-two feet to tiny ones smaller than a pencil. Most striking in the visual aspect of the organ are the fanfare trumpets proudly extending out above

Fig. 39: Organ builder Aidan Walsh prepares to install new organ pipes.

the center aisle at the front of the organ loft. In a bow to the past, 693 of the old pipes, both wood and metal, and a couple of the wind chests, were restored and incorporated into the new instrument, so that in the words of the builder, "the old organ is, in a sense, a reincarnation within the new." Another significant feature of the organ is the mechanical action of its keyboards, as opposed to electronic action, which is most common in this country. Mechanical action gives the organist a direct connection with the pipes, which allows a greater nuance of expressivity.[23]

As part of a special Vespers on May 20, 1993, the organ was first demonstrated by Cathedral organist Dr. Kenneth L. Udy and blessed by Bishop Weigand, with additional music by the Madeleine Choir School and the Cathedral Choir, both led by Gregory Glenn, and with greetings by the organ builder Kenneth L. Jones and donor Spencer F. Eccles. The following evening, in an Inaugural Recital, the organ was demonstrated again across the full spectrum of its capabilities by David Higgs, from the organ faculty of the Eastman School of Music in Rochester, New York. An Inaugural Organ Recital Series continued throughout the 1993–94 season with concerts by artists from England, Mexico, and Salt Lake City. That series became the annual Eccles Organ Festival, supported by the Eccles Foundation, the Utah Arts Council, the Salt Lake County Zoo, Arts, and Parks Fund, and donations from a Friends of the Eccles Festival organization. The festival is thus truly a community project which brings organists from around the world to Salt Lake City for an annual series of free public recitals.[24]

Upon the reopening of the Cathedral at the end of construction in 1993, the restored murals, woods, and glass mingled with the new stone work into a magnificent mosaic, brilliant in their new colors. Bishop Weigand acknowledged the widespread religious and civic support throughout the restoration at a gathering for Rededication of the Cathedral to Public Service on Saturday, February 20, 1993, at which President Thomas S. Monson of the First Presidency of the Church of Jesus Christ of Latter-day Saints also spoke. Mass for the dedication took place the next day, with Cardinal Roger Mahony of Los Angeles and Apostolic Pro-Nuncio Archbishop Agostino Cacciavillan present. On the following day, the Utah Chamber Artists presented a concert of thanksgiving, inaugurating a tradition of musical events that has brought every major performing arts organization in Utah to the Cathedral, including the Utah Symphony, Ballet West, the Utah Opera, and the Mormon Tabernacle Choir, as well as others from around the world.[25]

The motto for the Cathedral renovation, "A Cathedral for All People," pointed to the ways in which the Cathedral greatly expanded its civic role during the renovation period. "The Church and its liturgy do not exist in a place apart from the human city but as institutions in the midst of the city gracefully transfusing and redeeming its life," Msgr. Mannion has written.[26] In addition to the Eccles Organ Festival mentioned above, the Cathedral expanded its community role through the Good Samaritan Program, the Madeleine Festival of the Arts and Humanities, and the Madeleine Choir School.

The Good Samaritan Program, successor to the Community Ministries Program established by Msgr. William H. McDougall during his tenure as Cathedral rector from 1960 to 1980, achieved its greatest size from about 1986 to 2000. At its height, the program employed eighty-five volunteers working 7,500 hours annually and serving over 500 people weekly, "in the long tradition of local churches seeking to make a difference in their communities through practical charity in the name of Christ," as a brochure for the program put it. The breadth of services provided defy concise description. The free sack lunches were perhaps the most conspicuous service, but many others were less visible. Vouchers were available for gasoline, lodging, and prescriptions, while grocery delivery, yard work and rent and utility assistance were provided for the poor and the housebound. Others received clothing, counseling, referral to appropriate government and social services agencies, transportation and free long distance telephone calls. All services were free and dispensed with no questions asked; "we are committed to the service of all who seek help, regardless of religious background or affiliation," the brochure continued. Financial support for the program came from individual donations, the Utah Food Bank, area churches, and businesses and civic groups. The program's annual telethon and fund-raising dinner provided major support as did proceeds from the Poor Box at the rear of the Cathedral.

Though the Good Samaritan Program was an example of Christian charity at its finest, some well-heeled Avenues residents, including the mayor of the city, objected to the sometimes unsavory patrons it attracted, but Msgr. Mannion stood his ground, pointing out that the Cathedral is an inner city church, and that it was going to continue the Good Samaritan Program as long as he was rector. When the mayor objected that the Avenues was not zoned for charitable agencies, Msgr. Mannion countered that the Avenues was zoned for churches, and therefore it was zoned for charity.[27]

The Madeleine Choir School was created by Gregory Glenn. He was ideally suited to the project. A native of the State of Washington, Glenn completed his undergraduate degree in organ performance. His graduate degree at Catholic University was in theology with an emphasis on liturgical studies and included graduate work in choral conducting and Gregorian Chant studies. He came to Utah in 1988 to become the Diocesan Director of Liturgy, to which he added the position of Director of Liturgy and Music for the Cathedral in 1990, then transferred full time to the Cathedral in 1991.[28]

The Choir School began quite modestly on March 19, 1990 as an after school program for children with musical talent, who were invited to participate after taking an audition. The idea aroused considerable enthusiasm, and the initial Boy Choir and Girl Choir each had thirty-five members. As the program continued, Glenn began exploring the idea of a choir school on a European model. During the Cathedral renovation, he was able to spend two months in England, studying the choir school at Westminster Cathedral as a model for how one could be set up in Salt Lake City. "That time for me was invaluable," he recalled. "I think I learned more in that two months about some aspects of church music than I did in many of my courses in my undergraduate and graduate work." Upon his return, he had included in the renovation a restructuring of Scanlan Hall in the Cathedral basement as quarters for the school.[29]

When the school opened in 1996, it was full. The parents were taking a big risk, because they had to withdraw their children from the other Catholic schools in which they were enrolled, and take a chance that the Choir School would succeed, in the face of the fact that, as Glenn recalls, "We had no teachers, no principal, no desks, no books—nothing."[30] But they had the support of Bishop George H. Niederauer and Msgr. Mannion, they had the person of Glenn himself, with his tremendous work ethic and focus, they acquired a superb principal in Mrs. Elizabeth "Betsy" Hunt, and they had the enthusiasm of the students and the commitment of the parents.

Unfortunately, they did not have the unified support of the Catholic community nor the support of the other Catholic schools. Glenn was sometimes asked if the diocese really needed another Catholic school. His response was that the Choir School is a unique institution, and that while the diocese did not probably need another Catholic school, it did need a choir school. Part of the hostility, too, in Glenn's mind, was grounded in a certain philistinism that considers the arts as elitism. "We are hardly elitist," he objected. "That was something, to be honest, of a cheap shot taken at the arts. It's a very common criticism."[31] Eventually, of course, the Choir School became a dramatic success. Not only is the educational program of a very high quality, but the musical achievement of the children has enabled them to perform with every major musical organization in Utah, to sing at the 2002 Olympics, and to travel to France, Belgium, Germany, and Italy, where they performed for Pope John Paul II.

The school's basement quarters in the Cathedral were never adequate, with cramped space and no playground. In May 2002 the school was fortunate to be able to purchase the Avenues campus of the Episcopal Rowland Hall-St. Mark's school right across First Avenue from the Cathedral. The $1.4 million fundraising effort was largely the responsibility of Principal Betsy Hunt. The first million dollar gift came from Robert C. Steiner, whose wife, Jacqueline Erbin, had passed away in childbirth, so he had a great interest in children. One of the main buildings is named Jacqueline Erbin Hall. Another two million came from the McCarthy family under the leadership of Jane McCarthy (for whom the main classroom was named). The last million was raised by Bishop Niederauer from the Daniel Murphy Foundation. So, when the school moved into its new quarters late in 2006, it was debt-free.[32]

Music was not the only cultural activity featured in the Cathedral's public programs. In about 1986 the Cathedral began sponsoring an annual lecture in honor of Msgr. William H. McDougall. The program continued until 2000 and featured some distinguished speakers, one of the most eminent of whom was Mary Ann Glendon, Distinguished Professor of Law at Harvard and later American ambassador to the Holy See. She was coming to Brigham Young University to receive an honorary degree, and the Cathedral was able to get her to give a lecture there as well.[33]

In the spring of 1987 the Cathedral sponsored the first annual Madeleine Festival of the Arts and Humanities as an ongoing event during the Easter season. Building on the tradition, which began in the theatrical presentation marking the reopening of the Cathedral after the renovation under Bishop Federal, the Festival has included a wide variety of lectures, presentations, and performances. Much of the excellence of the

Fig. 40: Bishop John C. Wester.

festival can be attributed to the leadership of Marrie Hart of Ballet West, and more recently to Anne Collopy and Drew Browning. Each year the festival includes a Madeleine Award Dinner which honors members of the community who have contributed extensively to the arts. A notable fact about the festival is that it is entirely funded by outside sources like the Friends of the Madeleine Festival, the Salt Lake Arts Council, the Utah Arts Council, and the Salt Lake County Zoo, Arts, and Parks fund, with no Cathedral money involved. "It's really kind of a remarkable grass-roots effort," Gregory Glenn observed. "It's pretty amazing for what it accomplishes, given its small budget."[34]

Less than a year after the rededication of the restored Cathedral, on November 18, 1993, Bishop Weigand received word of his appointment by Pope John Paul II as bishop of Sacramento, California. A farewell Mass and an ecumenical banquet highlighted events honoring him on January 10, 1994. Bishop Weigand's fourteen years of episcopal leadership prepared the way for the growing diversity of the Catholic population that would increasingly enrich Utah culture. His fundraising success, creation of the Catholic Foundation (an endowment to support diocesan development), and establishment of parishes and missions, significantly built up the diocese. He left Salt Lake City among glowing tributes from Catholics as well as many other friends in the community he came to know during the Cathedral restoration.[35]

The Cathedral of the Madeleine has felt only a light touch from subsequent bishops, though of course it has remained the site of many inspiring liturgies and cultural events. A new chapter in the Cathedral's history was marked by the departure of Msgr. Mannion in 2000 to assume directorship of a newly created Mundelein Liturgical Institute in Chicago.[36] He was replaced by Father (later Monsignor) Joseph M. Mayo. Each rector of course leaves his own mark on the life of the parish. Like Msgr. Mannion, Msgr. Mayo understands the profound importance of liturgy, and in an attempt to connect modern parishioners with the rich traditions of the liturgy, he has introduced more Latin into the vernacular Mass, particularly the chanting of the Creed in Latin at the principal Sunday Mass. Perhaps even more importantly, he has created an endowment for ongoing maintenance of the Cathedral, supported by an annual Bishop's Dinner featuring a presentation of some theme in the history of the building. As the endowment grows, future bishops, rectors, and parishioners will have fewer anxieties about raising money to fix the deteriorating structure.

Another significant change at the Cathedral is the addition of a wildly popular Spanish Mass on Sunday afternoons. A Spanish choir, formed by Gregory Glenn, provides music for the overflowing congregation. Under the direction of parochial vicar, Father Omar Ontiveros, Hispanic pastoral ministry has been expanded with catechism classes, fiestas, and liturgical celebrations. Indeed, the Cathedral exists to serve all people.

On February 19, 2008, an event enabled all Cathedral parishioners to connect with their past. Working for an entire day, stonemasons from R. J. Enterprises in Heber City laboriously removed the time capsule that had been placed in the Cathedral cornerstone at the time of its installation in 1900. The following afternoon the diocesan archivist and Msgr. Mayo held their breaths in front of a crowd of onlookers and reporters in the Diocesan Pastoral Center as they removed the lid, then donned white archives gloves to remove the contents. To their surprise, they learned that in addition to a collection of coins, stamps, photographs and newspapers from 1900, the box contained additional artifacts from the Bishop Federal renovation in 1977. The capsule had been opened at that time, though no one alive then seemed to remember it, and no written record had been kept, other than an explanatory note within the box itself. The original box had been replaced at that time with an expensive airtight stainless steel box, and the contents deacidified by a rarely used process called vapor phase deacidification.[37]

The artifacts were then placed on public display, first in the Cathedral at a Mass in which Bishop John C. Wester cleverly tantalized onlooking Choir School children with images of pirates and buried treasure (subversively tricking them into developing an interest in history) and then in the Pastoral Center. Those who viewed the contents found that they inspired reflections on the state of the diocese at those two critical points in its history, as well as all other points in between and since, and the function of the Cathedral throughout that history and into the future. And, as preparations were made to reinstall the capsule during the celebration of the centennial of the Cathedral on August 15, 2009, thoughts naturally occur as to what should be placed in the capsule to represent our time and our engagement with that marvelous building. One thing is clear: like our predecessors going all the way back to Bishop Scanlan, our love for the great edifice is complex and powerful, and its significance for our spiritual lives is profound. As the Cathedral enters its second century, our prayers are for future Utah Catholics, that they will continue to love and care for it as we who came before them have done.

Fig. 41: Upper level of the apse before the scaffolding was removed in 1993.

Endnotes

Chapter 1

1. G. Clell Jacobs, "The Phantom Pathfinder: Juan Maria Antonio de Rivera and His Expedition," *Utah Historical Quarterly* 60 (Summer 1992): 200–223; Ted J. Warner, ed., *The Dominguez-Escalante Journal: Their Expedition Through Colorado, Utah, Arizona, and New Mexico in 1776* (Salt Lake City: University of Utah Press, 1995); David J. Weber, *The Taos Trappers: The Fur Trade in the Far Southwest, 1540–1846* (Norman: University of Oklahoma Press, 1971); James H. Knipmeyer, "Denis Julien: Midwestern Fur Trader," *Missouri Historical Review* 95 (April 2001): 245–63, and "The Denis Julien Inscriptions," *Utah Historical Quarterly* 64 (Winter 1966): 52–69; David E. Miller, "Peter Skene Ogden's Journal of His Expedition to Utah, 1825," *Utah Historical Quarterly* 20 (April 1952): 159–86.

2. Msgr. Jerome Stoffel, "The Hesitant Beginnings of the Catholic Church in Utah," *Utah Historical Quarterly* 36 (Winter 1968): 41–62. Fr. Keller's Masses would have been the first recorded ones in Utah history, as the friars Dominguez and Escalante left no record of celebrating Mass after they departed from Abiquiu, New Mexico.

3. *Ibid.*, 56; Msgr. Jerome Stoffel to Bernice Mooney, February, 1980, quoted on p. 3 of the first edition of this book; Father Denis Kiely, "A Brief History of the Church in Utah," 1900, MS in Diocesan Archives. The *Salt Lake Semi-Weekly Telegraph*, March 14, 1867, reports the arbitration of the matter and adds that Brigham Young even offered five hundred dollars toward construction of the school. Since the school was never built, the money never changed hands. The author is indebted to Ronald G. Watt for this reference.

4. *Salt Lake Tribune*, November 5, 1866.

5. Why St. Mary Magdalene? The answer can only be speculative, but it likely has something to do with the fact that her feast day, July 22, is the closest feast day of a major saint to July 24, which Utah celebrates as Pioneer Day to commemorate the entry of the first body of Mormon immigrants to Salt Lake Valley in 1847.

6. Until 1931 when the Diocese of Reno was created, the Diocese of Salt Lake included the entire territory and later state of Utah and the seven eastern counties of Nevada. (By papal decree in 1951, the name of the Diocese of Salt Lake was changed to the Diocese of Salt Lake City.)

7. This narrative of Bishop Scanlan's life is based mostly on Robert J. Dwyer, "Pioneer Bishop: Lawrence Scanlan, 1843–1915," *Utah Historical Quarterly* 20 (April 1952): 135–58; and Stasia Ryan to Bernice Mooney, August 29, 1979, letter in possession of Mrs. Mooney, but quoted in large part in the first edition of this book, pp. 5–6. Bishop Scanlan's mother and Miss Ryan's great-grandfather were siblings.

8. Dwyer, "Pioneer Bishop," 139.

9. *Ibid.*, 139–40.

10. *Ibid.*, 140.

11. Wain Sutton, ed., *Utah, A Centennial History* (New York: Lewis Historical Publishing Company, 1949): 2:744–54.

12. *Intermountain Catholic Register*, August 13, 1971.

13. John Bernard McGloin, "Two Early Reports Concerning Roman Catholicism in Utah, 1876–1881," *Utah Historical Quarterly* 29 (October 1961): 333–46; Father Francis J. Weber, "Father Lawrence Scanlan's Report of Catholicism in Utah, 1880," *Utah Historical Quarterly* 34 (Fall 1966): 283–89. See also McGloin, *California's First Archbishop: The Life of Joseph Sadoc Alemany, O.P., 1814–1888* (New York: Herder and Herder, 1966), pp. 124–25 on solicitation of funds from the Society. Although this book says little, if anything, specifically about Utah, it offers excellent background on general conditions in the archdiocese and its struggling Metropolitan Province.

14. Kiely, "Brief History," n.p.

15. "Historical Dates and Background Material," Cathedral of the Madeleine Archives. Lot 1, on which the present Bishop Hunt Center and the former convent called "Cobblecrest" are situated, were purchased in 1926 during the interregnum between Bishops Glass and Mitty by diocesan administrator Msgr. Patrick Cushnahan, using $25,520.83 of Metropolitan Life Insurance funds paid upon the death of Bishop Glass. Bernice Maher Mooney, *Salt of the Earth: The History of the Catholic Church in Utah, 1776–1987* (Salt Lake City: Catholic Diocese of Salt Lake City, 1987), p. 181. To round out the rest of the block, the south half of Lot 4 was purchased from the Culmer family in 1949 by Father Robert J. Dwyer, Rector of the Cathedral, and the Cathedral High School erected on that site. It was closed in 1970 and the building became the Diocesan Pastoral Center. *Ibid.*, p. 70; Diocesan property records, Diocesan Archives. In 2003 the diocese completed its ownership of the entire block by purchasing the William Culmer house, built by Utah artist H. L. A. Culmer for his older brother on the north half of Lot 4, from Mrs. Jane Stromquist. Diocesan property records, Diocesan Archives; Msgr. J. Terrence Fitzgerald and Bernice Maher Mooney, *Catholic Utah at the Turn of the Century, 1988–2002* (Salt Lake City: Catholic Diocese of Salt Lake City, 2003), pp. 101–2.

16. Bishop Scanlan used various sites for his rectory, beginning with the rooms in the back of St. Mary's church occupied in 1873. In 1887 he moved into rooms at All Hallows College until August 1889, when he moved to a building at 1st South and 3rd East, which he had planned to be the site of the new cathedral. In 1891 he was informed by an architect that the lot was too small for the cathedral, so he erected the present rectory and turned the previous building over to the new St. Ann's Orphanage. The orphans remained there until the Kearns-St. Ann's Orphanage on 21st South opened in 1899. Kiely, "Brief History," n.p.

17. Robert J. Dwyer, *The Gentile Comes to Utah: A Study in Religious and Social Conflict (1862–1890)* (Washington, D.C.: The Catholic University of America Press, 1941), 159; "Pioneer Bishop," p. 146.

18. Both the Gorlinski and Little stories appear in the first edition without attribution and are evidently based on Bernice Mooney's acquaintance with both people.

19. *Salt Lake Mining Review,* May 30, 1900.

20. "Complete Report of Expenditures by Bishop Scanlan on New Cathedral, July 4, 1899 to May 20, 1912," p. 63, Diocesan Archives.

21. Dwyer, "Pioneer Bishop," p. 154.

22. *Intermountain Catholic,* December 7, 1908.

23. *Salt Lake Daily Herald,* July 20, 1907; Robert J. Dwyer, "The Story of the Cathedral of the Madeleine," p. 23; Bernice Mooney to Joe Nerenberg, November 13, 1980, Diocesan Archives. Donors of windows in the baptistry are listed in the *Intermountain Catholic,* August 21, 1909.

24. *Intermountain Catholic,* August 14, 1909.

25. W. R. Harris, *The Catholic Church in Utah, 1776–1909* (Salt Lake City: The Intermountain Catholic Press, 1909).

26. Dwyer, "The Story of the Cathedral of the Madeleine," p. 11.

27. See photographs in the commemorative booklet in Diocesan Archives.

28. Dwyer, "Pioneer Bishop," pp. 152, 157.

29. *Intermountain Catholic,* December 29, 1906.

30. Rev. Louis J. Fries, *One Hundred and Fifty Years of Catholicity in Utah* (Salt Lake City: The Intermountain Catholic Press, 1926), 42.

Chapter 2

1. Rev. Stafford Poole, C.M., "'An Active and Energetic Bishop:' The Appointment of Joseph Glass, C.M. as Bishop of Salt Lake City," *Vincentian Heritage* 15(1994): 132–33. These reports reached Archbishop Patrick Riordan from none other than Thomas Kearns, a former Senator from Utah, publisher of the *Salt Lake Tribune,* and one of the wealthiest and most prominent Utah Catholics.

2. *Ibid.*, 152–53. Fr. Poole's article is highly recommended for anyone interested in the complex situation during Bishop Scanlan's last days and the appointment of Bishop Joseph S. Glass. Bishop Glass had actually been chosen as auxiliary, but upon Bishop Scanlan's death he was made the ordinary instead.

3. *Ibid.*, 120–21.

4. *Ibid.*, 123.

5. Margaret Leslie Davis, *Dark Side of Fortune: Triumph and Scandal in the Life of Oil Tycoon Edward L. Doheny* (Berkeley: University of California Press, 1998).

6. Bernardine Ryan Martin, Interview by Msgr. William H. McDougall, Jr., April 5, 1980, pp. 4, 7–8, 11, 13. Diocesan Archives.

7. Ralph Adams Cram, *Church Building* (Boston: Marshall Jones Co., 1924), 239, 320. Rev. Robert F. McNamara to Bishop Joseph Lennox Federal, June 25, 1975, Federal Papers, Diocesan Archives.

8. John Theodore Comes, *Catholic Art and Architecture: A Lecture to Seminarians* ([Pittsburgh:] The author, 1918), 5, 7, 10. Copy in Diocesan Archives. Psalm 126:1.

9. *Intermountain Catholic*, 26 March 1917, quoting the *Pittsburgh Sun*.

10. Although no adequate photographs of the windows have been found, that order is documented on the last page of a book in the Scanlan Papers in the Diocesan Archives labeled "Cathedral Building 1899–1904." A diagram in Bishop Glass's handwriting documents the removal of the three central windows, giving their subject and the name of the donors of all but the second one.

11. "An Old World Shrine in Salt Lake City," *Salt Lake Tribune*, November 4, 1917 reports conversations to that effect with Bishop Glass, John Theodore Comes, and artist Felix Lieftuchter.

12. The following information on Lieftuchter and his work comes mainly from Patricia R. McCoy's article in the *Salt Lake Tribune*, September 9, 1972, which in turn was based on notes from her interview with the artist and his response to a questionnaire sent him by Msgr. William H. McDougall, all of which are in the Lieftuchter file in Diocesan Archives.

13. Comes to Glass, April 18, 1917 in Comes file, Bishop Glass Papers, Diocesan Archives; "List of Bills Paid By Bishop Glass," in Bishop Glass Papers.

14. Mooney, *The Story of the Cathedral of the Madeleine*, p. 66.

15. Decker Little, a Salt Lake man who worked as Lieftuchter's assistant, recalls that the absorbent material was felt; Lieftuchter recalled it as cork. Little's reminiscences as reported to Bernice Mooney, are given in her *The Story of the Cathedral of the Madeleine*, p. 66.

16. Mooney, *The Story of the Cathedral of the Madeleine*, p. 66.

17. "An Old World Shrine in Salt Lake City," *Salt Lake Tribune*, November 4, 1917.

18. Rev. Robert H. Dwyer, *The Story of the Cathedral of the Madeleine*, Salt Lake City, Utah, 1866–1936 (n.p.; n.d.), 31.

19. This story comes from the recollections of Bernice Maher Mooney.

20. Rev. Robert F. McNamara to Bishop Joseph Lennox Federal, June 25, 1975.

21. Cram, *Church Building*, 228.

22. *Diocesan Monthly*, July, 1924, p. 7.

23. *Ibid.*, August, 1924, p. 5.

24. *Ibid.*, May, 1925.

Chapter 3

1. Fr. Robert J. Dwyer, a true "native" Utahn born and reared in Salt Lake City, was ordained to the priesthood in 1932, later becoming Bishop of Reno and Archbishop of Portland, Oregon, but he never served his native diocese as its bishop.

2. Bishop John J. Mitty to Patrick Cardinal Hayes, November 18, 1926, Mitty Papers, Diocesan Archives.

3. As May 14, 1928 was a Monday, one suspects that there were few attendees from outside Salt Lake City and perhaps Ogden and Park City.

4. These figures are found in Mooney, *Salt of the Earth*, p. 181. Dwyer went on to have a very distinguished career: after earning a Ph.D. in history and serving as a priest in the Diocese of Salt Lake City, he was ordained Bishop of Reno in 1952 and Archbishop of Portland, Oregon, in 1967. Albert J. Steiss, ed., *Ecclesiastes: The Book of Archbishop Robert J. Dwyer* (Los Angeles: National Catholic Register, 1982).

5. Mooney, *The Story of the Cathedral of the Madeleine*, 111–12.

6. *Ibid.*, 111.

7. *Intermountain Catholic*, April 16, 1932.

8. *Ibid.*, March 29, 1935.

9. *Ibid.*, January 18, 1935.

10. *Ibid.*, April 17, 1936.

11. *Ibid.*, November 13, 1936.

12. *Ibid.*, August 6, 1937.

13. *Intermountain Catholic Register*, April 22, 1960

14. Hunt, "My Conversion to the Catholic Faith," 2, pamphlet in the Hunt Papers, Diocesan Archives, originally published in *The Epistle of the St. Paul Guild*, January, 1949

15. *Ibid.*, 17.

16. *Ibid.*

17. *Ibid.*, 18–19.

18. *Ibid.*, April 22, 1960.

19. March 24, 1940. Bishop Hunt typed up the announcements for each Sunday Mass and had them bound into volumes, which included occasional letters to the people of the Cathedral which he directed to be read at the same time. Those bound volumes are in the Diocesan Archives.

20. *Ibid.*, August 7 and 22, October 10, 1940; June 18 and July 7, 1941; July 5 and September 14, 1944.

21. The parish announcements for December 14, 1941 (the first Sunday after the attach on Pearl Harbor) included an uncited newspaper article by the bishop which includes the quotation given here. The Honor Roll for the Cathedral hung in the church until it began to deteriorate, and is now housed in the Diocesan Archives. There is also a photograph album of Cathedral service people, with the notation "Killed in action" after several of the photographs. The communion announcement was dated December 27, 1941.

22. Parish announcements, February 14, 1943.

23. *Ibid.*, May 4, 1944.

24. *Ibid.*, August 12, 1945.

25. The Diocesan Archives contains missals in a special large, bold type which Bishop Hunt used to continue saying Mass after his vision began to fail.

Chapter 4

1. *Intermountain Catholic Register*, February 25, 1951 gives a concise biographical sketch of Bishop Federal to the time of his consecration.

2. *Ibid.*

3. *Ibid.*, April 22, 1951. I have supplied the Utah population figure.

4. *Salt Lake Tribune*, October 14, 1967.

5. *The Register Supplement*, September 7, 1979.

6. Msgr. Francis J. Weber, *St. Viviana's Cathedral, a Centennial History* (Los Angeles: The author, 1976).

7. Gary Topping, *"If I Get Out Alive:" World War II Letters and Diaries of William H. McDougall, Jr.* (Salt Lake City: University of Utah Press, 2007).

8. *Salt Lake Tribune*, June 29, 1980.

Chapter 5

1. *Intermountain Catholic*, May 20, 1988.

2. *Salt Lake Tribune*, November 19, 1980.

3. These symbols are explained in a document by the designer of the coat of arms, Paul J. Sullivan, in the Weigand Papers, Diocesan Archives.

4. *Salt Lake Tribune*, August 11, 2007. See also *Sacramento Bee*, March 27, 2005 and December 24 and 25, 2005, copies in Weigand Papers, Box 265.3B2, Diocesan Archives.

5. The project is documented in the Records of the Cathedral of the Madeleine Interior Restoration/Renovation, 1987–1994, in the Diocesan Archives.

6. Interview with Msgr. M. Francis Mannion, February 4, 2009, p. 2, Diocesan Archives.

7. Msgr. M. Francis Mannion, "Public Church, Public Support: A Case Study in Ecclesiastical Fund Raising," address given to a plenary session of the Partners for Sacred Places National Conference, July 19, 1992, p. 3, Diocesan Archives. Mannion further developed his ideas on the relationship between church and community in "The Church and the City," *First Things* 100 (February 2000): 31–36

8. Mannion interview, pp. 11, 18.

9. *Ibid.*, pp. 4, 12.

10. Renovation records, Boxes VIII–XII.

11. *Ibid.*, Box II, Folder 5f.

12. Mannion interview, p. 10.

13. *Ibid.*, p. 8.

14. *Ibid.*, p. 21. Interview with Gregory Glenn, February 19, 2009, p. 2, Diocesan Archives.

15. Mannion interview, pp. 20–21; Glenn interview, p. 8.

16. Mannion interview, p. 6.

17. *Ibid.*, pp. 14–15. In order to placate people for whom the Veronica episode was a favorite, she was incorporated into the Station where Simon the Cyrene carries the cross.

18. Robert J. Dwyer, "Pioneer Bishop: Lawrence Scanlan, 1843–1915," *Utah Historical Quarterly* (April, 1952): 158.

19. Glenn interview, pp. 11–12; Mannion interview, p. 15.

20. Documentation on the Fairbanks donation is in the "Art" file in Diocesan Archives; Vern G. Swanson, Robert S. Olpin, and William C. Seifrit, *Utah Painting and Sculpture* (Salt Lake City: Gibbs Smith, 1991, 1997), p. 188.

21. Renovation records, Box XV, Folder 43.

22. Glenn interview, pp. 2–5.

23. Kenneth Jones, "Statement by the Organbuilder," an appendix to the program for the liturgy of the blessing of the organ, May 20, 1993, Diocesan Archives; Glenn interview, pp. 3–4.

24. Glenn interview, pp. 4–5.

25. Renovation records, Box XVI.

26. Mannion, "The Church and the City," p. 32.

27. "Caring for the City: The Good Samaritan Program at The Cathedral of the Madeleine," brochure in Diocesan Archives. The controversy over the program is based on the author's recollections and conversation with Msgr. Mannion, February 4, 2009.

28. Glenn interview, p. 1.

29. *Ibid.*, pp. 5–6, 8.

30. *Ibid.*, p. 6.

31. *Ibid.*

32. *Ibid.*, p. 8.

33. Mannion interview, p. 18.

34. Glenn interview, p. 9.

35. Weigand Papers, Box 265.3B2, Folders 65.1–2.

36. Msgr. Mannion, letter to Cathedral parishioners, December 8, 1999, Cathedral collection, Diocesan Archives.

37. *Salt Lake Tribune*, February 23, 2008; *Intermountain Catholic*, February 29, 2008.

Index

Agrell, Ian, 86

Alemany, Archbishop Joseph Sadoc, 3, 5

Architectural Planning Committee, 78

Aretz, Francis, 26

Aures, Walter, 33

Bambach, Phillip, 33

Barbacci, Norma, 80

Beyer Blinder Belle, 79

Bishops' Memorial, 86

Blessed Sacrament Chapel, 80, 86

Browning, Drew, 94

Cacciavillan, Archbishop Agostino, 91

Cathedral of the Madeleine; altar, 15–16; altar replaced, 85; ambry, 88; architects, 13–14, 24–25, 79; architectural style, 12, 13–14; baptismal font replaced, 86; bells installed; by Bishop Glass, 32; by Bishop Weigand, 88; Cathedral Restoration Drive, 65–66; confessionals altered, 88–89; construction of, 13–16; construction of rectory, 10; debt retired on, 50–51; decoration, 15–16; dedication, 17–19; designated Historical Site, 65; during World War II, 55–56; exterior changes under Bishop Glass, 25–26; exterior erosion, 65; funding from Pious Fund, 12–13; gargoyles installed, 33–34; groundbreaking, 12; interior changes under Bishop Glass, 26–33; interior lighting, 69–70; interior repairs, 69–71; Magdalen Room, 88; murals, 27–30; new organ, 89; organ modifications, 32–33; Our Lady of Zion chapel, 88; purchase of land for, 10; rededication, 1936, 50–51; renovation; under Bishop Federal, 64–71; under Bishop Glass, 25–33; replacement of finials, 66–67; restoration funding, 72; sculptures within, 30–31; sedilla, 88; Spanish Mass, 96; stained glass windows, 68, 81–83, 88; installed, 16; Stations of the Cross, 30, 83–84; symbolism within, 35–36; theatrical performance in, 71; time capsule, 96; tympanum, 25–26; vandalism in, 71

Cathedral Preservation Fund, 79

Cathedral Restoration Drive, 65–66

Catholic-Mormon relations, 11, 18

Collopy, Anne, 94

Comes, John Theodore, 24–25

Connor, Gen. Patrick E., 3

Cumming, Ian M., 78

Cummings, John B., 78–79

Doheny, Edward L., 23

Dominguez, Fray Atanasio, 1

Dominguez-Escalante expedition, 1

Dwyer, Fr. Robert J. (later
    Archbishop), 33, 45, 88

Eccles, George S. and Dolores Doré
    Foundation, 89–90

Eccles, Spencer F., 89

Eccles Organ Festival, 77, 90

Escalante, Fray Silvestre Velez de, 1

Fairbanks, Avard T., 88

Federal, Bishop Joseph Lennox;
    and Cathedral Restoration
    Drive, 65–66; and Vatican II,
    62–63; as Coadjutor Bishop,
    57; background and ordination,
    59–60; condition of diocese when
    ordained, 60–61; renovation of
    Cathedral, 64–71; restoration
    funding by, 72; retirement, 72–73

Fitch, James, 79

Foley, Fr. James, 3

Gallivan, John W., 73, 78

gargoyles, 33–34, 68

Gibbons, James Cardinal, 17–18, 19

Glass, Bishop Joseph Sarfield; ad
    limina visit, 38–39; and Doheny
    family, 23, 34; appraisal of,
    34; arrival in Salt Lake City,
    23–24; art works acquired
    by, 38–39; background and
    personality, 21–22; contrasted
    with Bishop Scanlan, 21–22;
    death and funeral, 39; diocesan

accomplishments of, 37–39;
    episcopal ordination, 23; financial
    skill of, 22–23; plans Cathedral
    renovation, 24–26; purchases his
    own home, 24

Glendon, Mary Ann, 94

Glenn, Gregory; and Bishop
    Scanlan's tomb, 85–86; and
    Madeleine School Choir, 92–95;
    background, 81, 92

Hanna, Archbishop Edward, 18

Hard Hat party, 81

Harris, Dean W. R., 17

Hart, Marrie, 94

Hayes, Ellen, 88

Heinz, Ethel Hogan Hanson.
    See Merrill, Ethel Hogan Hanson
    Heinz

Higgs, David, 90

Howa, Richard, 78

Hunt, Bishop Duane G., 41; and
    World War II, 55–56; background
    and conversion, 52–54; death
    of, 57; eye problems, 53, 56–57;
    ordination as priest and bishop,
    54–55; personality, 55

Hunt, Elizabeth "Betsy", 93

Huntsman, Jon M., Sr., 78

Johnson, Deacon Lynn, 85

Jones, Kenneth L., 90

Judge, John and Mary, 7

Kearney, Bishop James E.; appointed
    to Rochester, New York, 51;
    background and personality,
    47–50; retires Cathedral debt, 50

Kearns, Thomas, 7

Keiffer, Richard, 78

Keller, Fr. Bonaventure, 1

Kelly, Fr. Edward, 3

Kiely, Fr. Denis, 7, 21

Kingston, M. Ray, 78

Kirchmayer, Isaac, 32

Lieftuchter, Felix, 27–30

Little, Decker, 12

Lowell School, 81

Madeleine Choir School, 77, 92–94

Madeleine Festival of the Arts, 77, 94–95

Magdalen Room, 88

Mahony, Cardinal Roger, 91

Mannion, Msgr. M. Francis; as "renovation bureaucrat", 78; background and appointment as rector, 77; departure for Chicago, 95; quoted, 81

Mayo, Msgr. Joseph M., 95

McCance, Murray, 86

McDougall, Msgr. William H., 62, 66, 91

McDougall Lecture Series, 77, 93

Mecklenburg, Bernard R., 15

Merrill, Ethel Hogan Hanson Heinz, 33, 38

Mitty, Bishop John J.; and diocesan indebtedness, 42–46; appointed to San Francisco, 47; appraisal of, 45–47; background and ordination, 41–42; meeting with heads of households, 44–45

Monson, President Thomas S., 90

Morgan, Roger, 85

mountain men, 1

Neuhausen, Carl M., 13–14

O'Donnell, Neil, 85

Ontiveros, Fr. Omar, 96

Our Lady of Zion chapel, 88

Pious Fund of the Californias, 12

Raverdy, Fr. John Batiste, 3

Rivera, Juan Maria Antonio de, 1

Rohlf's Stained and Leaded Glass, 82–83

Scanlan, Bishop Lawrence, 41; and fundraising, 9; appointed Vicar Apostolic, 9–10; at Pioche, 5–6; biography of, 4–7; death and interment of, 18–19; episcopal ring of, 18; last years of, 21; sarcophagus moved, 85–86; sarcophagus of, 4

Schmitt, Henry, 30

Society for the Propagation of the Faith, 9

St. Mary's church, 6–10; closed and sold, 15; construction of, 3

stained glass windows, 68; donors of, 16; installation of, 16; removal of, 26–27, 81–83

Stations of the Cross; replaced by Bishop Glass, 30; replaced by Bishop Weigand, 83–84

Steck, Bishop Leo J., 57

Stoffel, Msgr. Jerome, 1

Sweeney, Irene, 78

Tremblay, Amedee, 38

Udy, Dr. Kenneth L., 90

"Vatican II" windows, 88

Vatican Council II, 62–63

Walsh, Fr. Patrick, 3

Weigand, Bishop William K.; appointment to Sacramento, California, 94; appraisal of, 94; as fundraiser, 79; background and ordination, 75–76; personality, 77

Wester, Bishop John C., 96

Wilson, Roger "Sam", 83–84

World War II, 55–56

Young, Brigham, 3

Zettler, Francis X., 16